MURDER

IN

VISALIA

MURDER IN VISALIA

THE COIN DEALER KILLER

RONN M. COUILLARD
Foreword by Terry Ommen

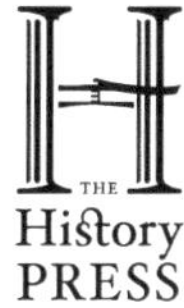

Published by The History Press
Charleston, SC
www.historypress.net

First published 2017

Manufactured in the United States

ISBN 9781625859808

Library of Congress Control Number: 2017940961

Notice: The information in this book is true and complete to the best of our knowledge. It is offered without guarantee on the part of the author or The History Press. The author and The History Press disclaim all liability in connection with the use of this book.

CONTENTS

FOREWORD

In 1979, Visalia was a sleepy, off-the-beaten-path town with loads of charm. Valley oak trees towered over the landscape, Mill Creek meandered its way through the downtown business district and historic buildings lined the streets, all combining to give the town a serene, almost idyllic feel. But on October 6, the serenity was shattered by the ruthless and violent murder of coin dealer Alex Moyer. His life was taken in his small shop not by a Visalia thug but rather by a killer from Fresno, the big city to the north.

Killings, especially those with perpetrators not in custody, have a way of stirring a town and leaving the citizens with an uneasy feeling. I was a sergeant with the Visalia Police Department at the time but had nothing to do with the investigation, so I really didn't get involved with the case.

But retired Superior Court judge and former Tulare County prosecutor Ronn Couillard did get to know the case very well, and thanks to him, we have *Murder in Visalia: The Coin Dealer Killer*, an extremely accurate and well-documented account of the crime and its successful prosecution.

Couillard at the time was a tough, no-nonsense Tulare County deputy district attorney who wasn't timid about tackling difficult cases, especially circumstantial ones. His keen memory, knowledge of the case and willingness to share make him the perfect person to pen this story. He has cleverly packed this volume with historic details, courtroom strategy and humor. It is easy to read, informative and entertaining.

At times, *Murder in Visalia* is intense, like when the convicted murderer was given a new trial by the Appeals Court. At other times, Couillard uses humor to describe the unusual but lawful tactics employed by investigators. When it is important for the reader to understand critical courtroom and criminal justice procedures, his explanations are concise and understandable even for the layperson.

If you like California history, especially that pertaining to Tulare County and Visalia, or if you like investigative sleuthing or courtroom drama, this fast-moving book is sure to please.

TERRY L. OMMEN
Retired Police Captain, Visalia Police Department
Historian and author, *Wild Tulare County: Outlaws, Rogues & Rebels*

ACKNOWLEDGEMENTS

Any prosecutor knows that you cannot do it alone. Everyone needs a team of dedicated people around to help ensure a successful conviction, particularly in a difficult case. That was exactly what we had in the Tulare County District Attorney's Office during my time there. The valued assistance of law clerks, secretaries, witness coordinators, investigators and fellow attorneys made matters significantly smoother and easier when engaged in a major jury trial. I was fortunate to work with a special group of people in that office between 1980 and 1987.

The success of this case was also brought about by the hard work and determination put forth by the detectives working these two coin dealer homicides, most notably Gary Snow and John Reynolds of the Fresno Police Department and Bill Wittman and Bill McGowen of the Visalia Police Department. They unhesitatingly ran down and investigated every potential lead and willingly pursued any investigative request that I had. These four were the real heroes in this prosecution.

I would also like to thank my friends at the Exeter Writers Guild. It was their patience and knowledge that made possible my being able to put this story together. They helped guide me through organizing and assembling the material, sentence structure and punctuation. Thank you all.

A special thank-you goes to retired police captain Terry Ommen for writing the foreword to this book. Terry was a well-respected police officer with the Visalia Police Department. He also is a noted historian and author on the history of Visalia and Tulare County.

Last but most certainly not least, I want to acknowledge my wife, Charlotte. Her patience, understanding and unwavering support made all of this possible, not only in the writing of the story but also way back at the beginning. During the early investigation and filing stage, as well as throughout the various court proceedings, she was always there to listen and offer common-sense advice and suggestions. She truly was a most valuable component to any success I may have had.

AUTHOR'S NOTE

This is the true story of a murder that I prosecuted as a deputy district attorney for Tulare County, California. The people, events, actions and conversations depicted within the story have been taken from police reports, court documents, recorded conversations, press accounts and my personal knowledge and interviews of the participants. To safeguard the privacy of certain people, some individuals' names and identifying characteristics have been changed.

INTRODUCTION

Visalia was the home of some forty thousand inhabitants in 1980. Located in California's fertile San Joaquin Valley, Visalia is the county seat of Tulare County, which along with adjoining counties combines to form one of the nation's richest agricultural areas. Known for searing summer heat and the famous Tule Fog in winter, Tulare County is a major producer of cotton, grapes, tree fruit, nuts and dairy products.

Located just beyond the foothills at the east end of the county is Sequoia National Park. Known as the Gateway to the Sequoias, Visalia was by far the largest city in Tulare County.

Visalia had shown slow yet steady growth during the 1970s. Its industry reflected the agricultural economic base, being the home to food processing plants, truck and tractor sales and service and other related service industries. A midwesterner would find Visalia typical of many towns of its size throughout Middle America. Although growing steadily in population, it had not yet exploded with the urban sprawl seen in neighboring cities like Fresno, forty-five miles to the north, and Bakersfield, some seventy-five miles to the south. Located eight miles east of Highway 99, one of California's major north–south arteries, a traveler using Highway 99 would not normally pass through Visalia, thereby leaving it relatively unknown.

As with other cities of similar or larger size in California, Visalia was beset by shopping malls and fast-food establishments. For the most part, however, these were located south of the original business district. Through the restoration of many of the original buildings and older homes, the central city had maintained the charm and attractiveness that many communities lose in their mad rush to commercialization. The population growth since the 1970s, though amazing to longtime residents, was modest by California standards. Determined not to lose their quality of life, Visalians, many of whom were transplanted from Southern California, kept a watchful eye on attempts to change the landscape from farms and groves to industrial parks, shopping centers and housing tracts, as had occurred throughout Los Angeles and Orange Counties.

Blessed with long, warm summers, Visalians enjoyed the outdoor life. Swimming pools were plentiful even in the more modest housing areas and, along with outdoor barbecuing, provided residents with a casual, informal lifestyle. Visalians loved baseball. The proud possessor in 1980 of the only city-owned professional baseball team in America, the Class A Visalia Oaks, they were vocal and spirited in support of their beloved Oaks. The parks, playgrounds and high school fields were overflowing with Little League and Babe Ruth baseball, as well as men's and women's fast- and slow-pitch softball leagues.

In 1980, I had been an attorney for some twelve years. I had been employed as a deputy district attorney with the Los Angeles County District Attorney's Office for more than nine years and had been in the private practice of law for almost three years.

In the spring of 1980, my law partner and I dissolved our law practice and went our separate ways. At the time, I was faced with several options, one of which was to finally move from the smog and congestion of Southern California. My wife, Charlotte, and I discussed it and chose to move if we could find the right situation.

In May 1980, I interviewed with Will Richmond, the district attorney of Tulare County. He called me a few weeks later and offered me a job, and my wife and I decided to make the move.

On Monday, June 16, 1980, I started employment as a deputy district attorney for Tulare County. At that time, the office had just undergone some turnover in personnel, and most of the attorneys were relatively inexperienced. With my background and experience, I was soon put in charge of the team of attorneys handling all cases arising in the Visalia Judicial District.

Having been born, raised and lived in heavily populated Los Angeles County, the chance to live and work in a small-town atmosphere was something Charlotte and I looked forward to. Although it was difficult to leave family and friends and relocate, we were not disappointed. We found that we traded the impersonal, rapid-paced, hustle and bustle of the megalopolis for the individuality and congeniality of the slower-paced, rural-type environment. Nowhere was this more evident than in the District Attorney's Office. Having previously been a deputy district attorney for more than nine years in Los Angeles County, when I left, that office employed in excess of 550 deputies. Now I was one of 23 deputies in the Tulare County office. This was analogous to being one of several hundred persons employed on an assembly line at General Motors and suddenly operating your own one-person auto repair business.

Not only was the difference in the size of the offices significant, but the county population differences were staggering as well. Tulare County was home at the time to approximately 200,000 people, whereas Los Angeles County was home to more than 7 million. The Los Angeles–Orange County Basin totaled a population in excess of 14 million.

Because of this difference in size, what tends to be routine and commonplace in the heavily populated areas becomes headline news in a smaller county or town. Nowhere is this more apparent than with the crime of murder. Considering that at the time, the city of Visalia had approximately three to four homicides per year, and the entire county eight to twelve, the newspapers would intently follow and report the developments in each case. The news stories supplied a chronicle of the crime, the filing of charges by the district attorney and the various court proceedings. From my experience, this aspect of the job of prosecutor was new and, I must admit, exciting.

Part I
THE VISALIA COIN DEALER MURDER

Finding the Victim

Barbara Heslinga pressed her face against the glass door of the small coin shop and peered inside. "I still don't see him," she said. Her husband, Dale, who was also looking through the glass door, replied, "There must be something wrong. Maybe he had a heart attack."

Their concern had begun the evening before, on Saturday, October 6, 1979. When they returned home shortly after 8:00 p.m. that evening, they found a notice from the city on their front door informing them to keep all vehicles off the street the following Monday, as some road resurfacing work was scheduled to be done.

The Heslingas lived in a small residence on Dudley Street in Visalia, California. Dudley Street is a short, north–south street that forms a T-intersection with Murray Street. Their house was adjacent to the back side of the U.S. Stamp and Coin Shop located at the northeast corner of Dudley and Murray. The coin shop was one of eight small shops housed in a single-story concrete-block building that fronted on Murray Street. The shop was located at the west end of the building nearest the intersection of Dudley and Murray.

Because of their limited driveway and garage space, Dale parked his pickup truck on the street in front of their home. Upon reading the notice, they decided to check with the coin shop operator for permission to park the

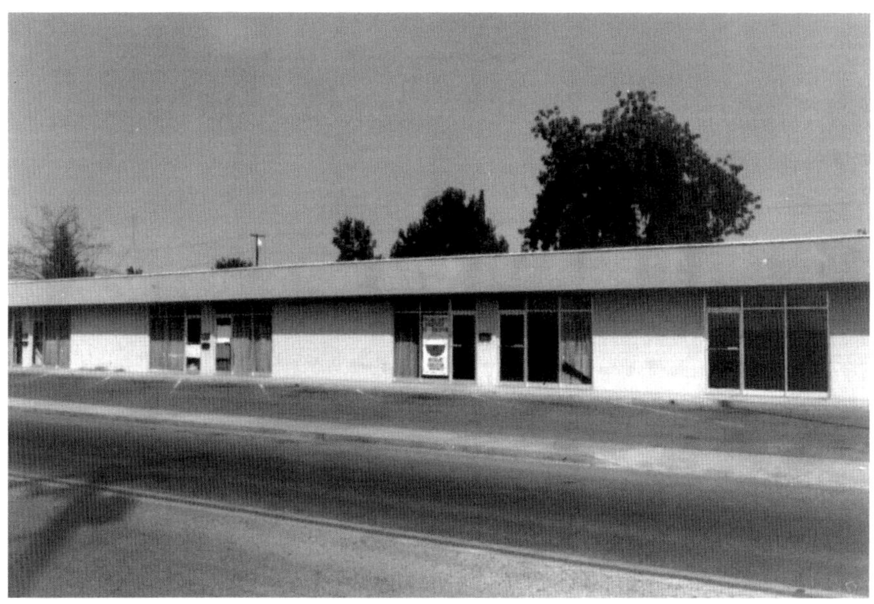

Murray Street looking at cement building, with coin shop at far left of photo. *Courtesy of Visalia Police Department.*

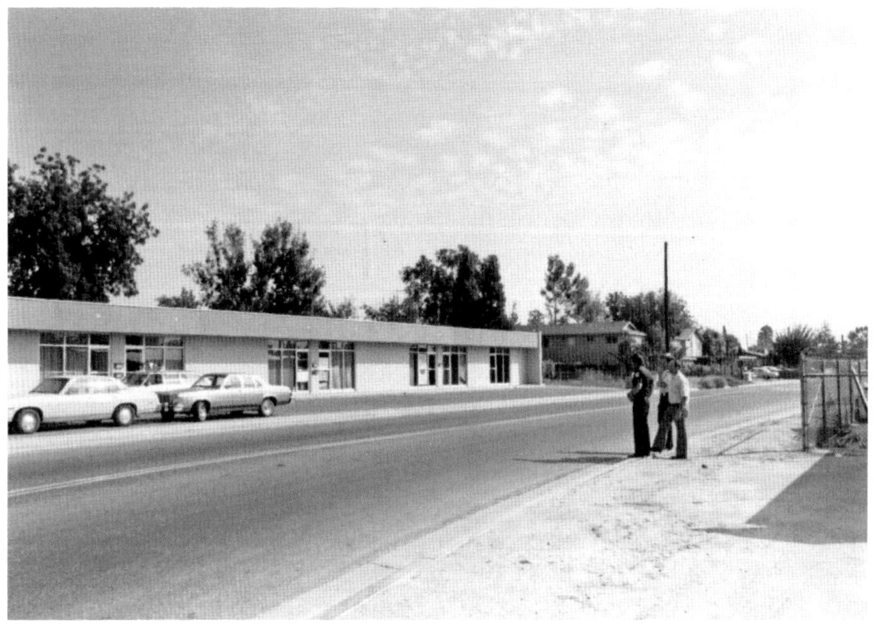

View of cement block building from south side of Murray Street. *Courtesy of Visalia Police Department.*

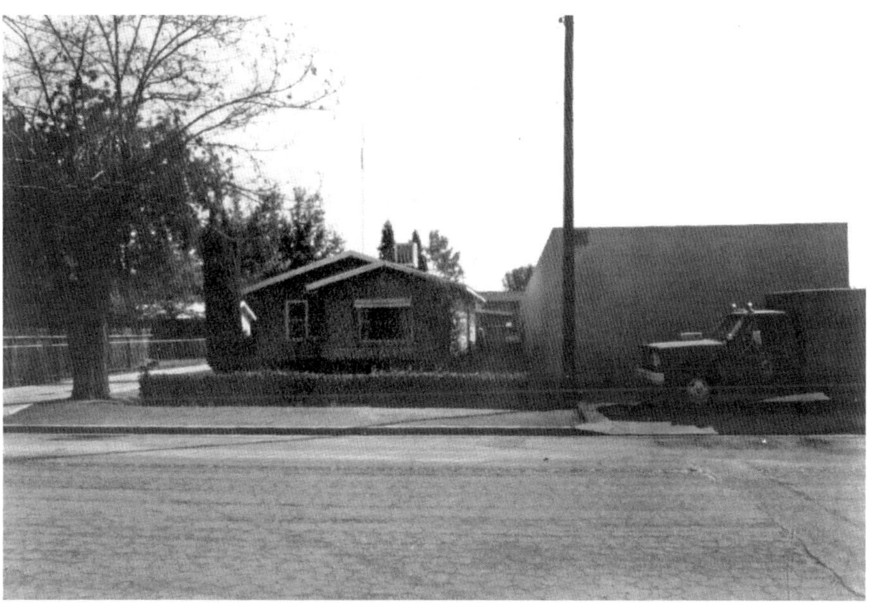

Heslinga residence on Dudley Street adjacent to back of coin shop. The police truck is parked where blue Cadillac is normally parked. *Courtesy of Visalia Police Department.*

truck in his parking lot that Monday. Since they had noticed the lights on in the coin shop and the familiar blue Cadillac driven by the shop's owner, Alex Moyer, parked in front of the shop upon their arrival home, they decided to contact him that Saturday evening.

It was about 8:30 p.m. when they walked around the corner to the coin shop and, finding the door locked, knocked. Receiving no response, they looked through the glass door and observed no one inside and nothing unusual. Although his lack of response caused them some concern, they concluded Mr. Moyer must have temporarily left with someone since it was well after normal business hours.

The next morning, Barbara Heslinga had gone out front to pick up the Sunday paper when she noticed the blue Cadillac parked in the same location. After telling her husband, they decided they would investigate further. Again, they peered through the glass door and viewed the same scene from the evening before. Just as they were about to leave, Dale walked to a window adjacent to the glass door. This window was covered with wooden louvers to prevent a view inside the shop. However, Dale

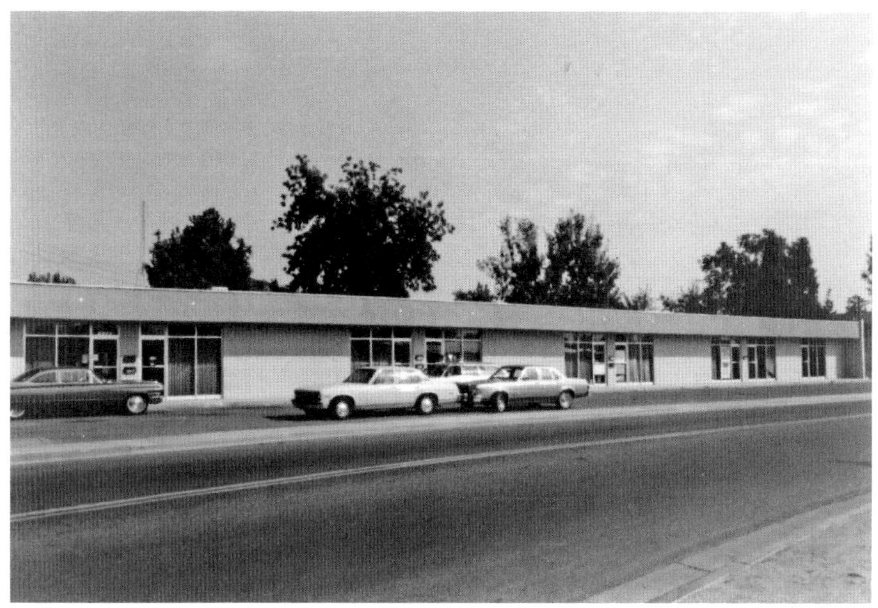

Murray Street looking at coin shop. The blue Cadillac is parked in front of the coin shop but not the normal location. *Courtesy of Visalia Police Department.*

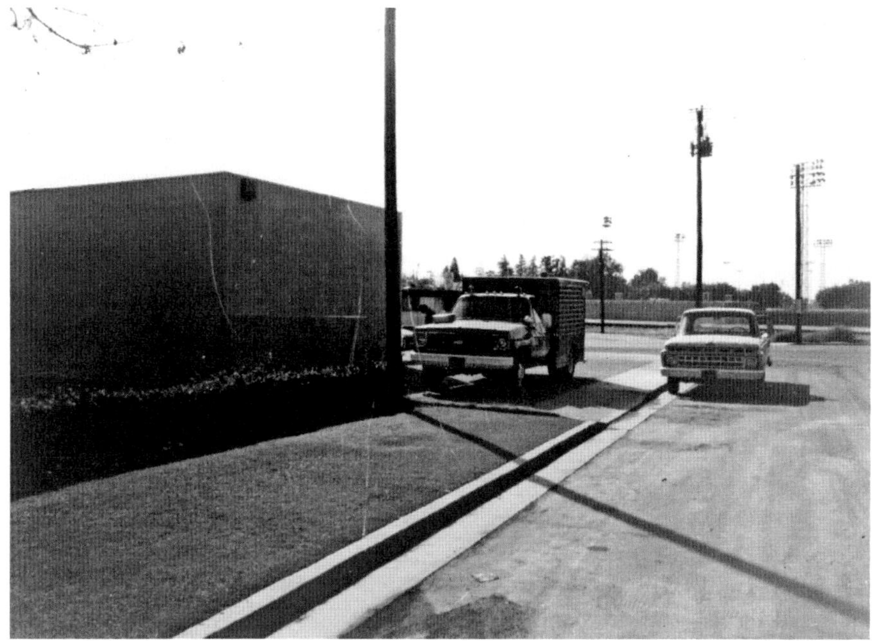

Side of coin shop. The police truck is parked where the blue Cadillac is normally parked. *Courtesy of Visalia Police Department.*

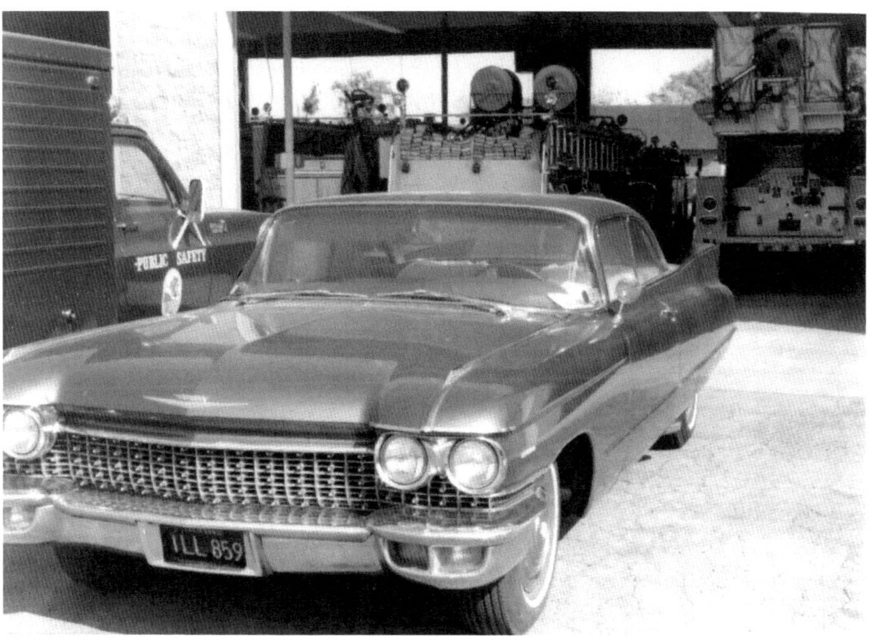

Alex Moyer's blue Cadillac at the police station. *Courtesy of Visalia Police Department.*

noticed a small opening in the louvers a few inches in width at the end of the window farthest from the door. Looking through this small opening, Dale noticed something. "Look, Barbara. Behind the counter to the far back. Isn't that his hat?"

Barbara moved to where Dale was standing and looked through the opening. "It sure looks like it," she exclaimed, "I've never seen him without it on. She surveyed the shop as best she could through the small opening and saw what appeared to be a person's arm on the floor extending out from behind the counter.

Fearing the worst, they called the police and told them of their discovery. The police and an ambulance arrived, and the door was opened by using a specially designed power saw to cut the deadbolt lock. As the police and paramedics entered the premises, Officer Hector Torres noticed that the alarm system did not activate, indicating that it may have been turned off. Officer Bobby Curtis checked the premises for possible suspects as Officer Torres proceeded behind the counter.

The body of Alex Moyer was lying facedown with both legs and left arm extended; his right arm was bent and underneath his chest area. Beneath his

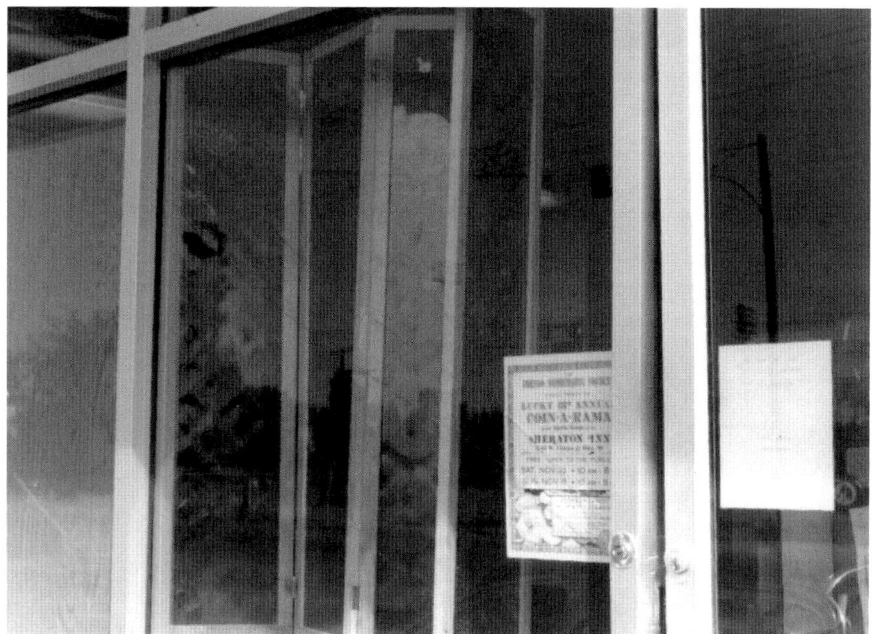

Glass windows and door to coin shop, with wooden louvers on windows. *Courtesy of Visalia Police Department.*

head was a pool of blood. The body was fully clothed with a multicolored red, white and blue plaid short-sleeve shirt, light khaki-colored slacks, a brown belt, brown shoes and rust-colored socks. Bloodstains were visible on the upper-left back area of the shirt.

Officer Torres assisted the paramedics in rolling Moyer's body over and checking for signs of life. It was cold and stiff to the touch. No signs of life were detected, and they rolled the body back to the position in which it was found. Officer Curtis called the station to inform the homicide detectives of the situation, while Officer Torres took the necessary steps to preserve the scene. He ushered the paramedics outside and positioned himself at the door to prevent anyone from entering as he awaited the arrival of the homicide investigators.

The Crime Scene

"Where's ID," growled John Calvin, referring to the Identification Bureau. "Those bastards are always late." John was a grizzled veteran of twenty-seven years, and as a homicide detective, it was readily apparent who was in charge of the investigation. Born in the Midwest, he left home after high school to join the U.S. Navy. After a four-year tour, he was discharged on June 24, 1950, the day the Korean War broke out. Rather than return to the sultry summers and cold winters of his home state, he decided to "have a ball in sunny California." However, the women and bars of San Diego soon made quick work of the small savings he had accumulated, and he suddenly found himself in need of a job.

After drifting from job to job, he began looking for something with more of a future. He found what appeared to be such an occupation when he was hired as a deputy sheriff for Kern County, California, of which Bakersfield is the county seat. John worked the jail and patrol for five years when he heard of, and applied for, a position as a police officer for the city of Visalia, located some seventy-five miles north of Bakersfield. He was hired, and after working patrol for several years, he was assigned to the detective division initially investigating burglaries and thefts.

The past twelve years as a homicide and violent crimes investigator, being called out in the middle of the night and experiencing the frustration attendant in the long hours of checking out endless leads, had taken its toll. He had ulcers and high blood pressure, both of which were aggravated by smoking two packs of cigarettes a day and drinking coffee excessively. John Calvin was the prototype of the tough, crusty cop portrayed in the movies. With the grease spot on his tie, white socks and blustering manner, he appeared to be bumbling and awkward, yet he got results, as evidenced by his rate of cases solved. He swore and cursed, badgered witnesses, intimidated subordinates and hated and bad-mouthed defense attorneys, yet he was effective and respected by his peers. What he lacked in formal education and diplomacy, he more than made up for with plain old hard work and common sense.

As the chief homicide investigator, he immediately and clearly took command. He ordered Curtis to secure the building within which the coin shop was located and Torres to diagram the shop. His assistant, Detective Bill McGowen, was directed to search the shop. Meanwhile, Calvin checked under and around the body and found no weapons. On the left side of the victim's back, the shirt was blood-soaked, and he noted small holes that appeared to be bullet wounds. In the victim's rear pants pocket, he found a wallet containing $211 in U.S. money, numerous credit cards and a driver's license. The driver's license was for a Frank Alexander Moyer Jr., with an address in Exeter, a small town some twelve miles east of Visalia. A roll of quarters was found open and lying a few inches from the body.

The coin shop was a small room with a customer counter on the east side of the room running in a north–south direction. This customer counter had a glass-covered display case at the top, and on the inside, away from the customer, there were several drawers. On the wall behind the counter were wooden shelves. At the south wall was the only door to the shop, along with two large windows covered with wooden louvers. Two desks were in the shop, one in the southwest corner and one at the far north end of the counter. A large table was next to the desk in the southwest corner. There was a small enclosed bathroom in the northwest corner of the premises.

The most striking part of the coin shop was the vast amount of memorabilia posted on the walls, sitting on shelves and exhibited in display cases. Frank Alexander Moyer Jr. was a collector. He had posters from World War I and II—some appealing to young men to join the military and others urging people to buy war bonds. There were USO-Canteen posters and other posters that prompted civilians to do their part for the war effort by growing victory gardens, conserving gas and so on. He had trinkets and objects from world fairs, old campaign and advertising posters and buttons and an assortment of stamps and coins mounted in display cases. In addition, there were papers and pamphlets on coins and stamps lying on the table and desks. Only the glass top of the counter was free of miscellaneous debris.

A short while later, an officer from the Identification Bureau arrived and began processing the scene by taking photographs, dusting for prints and collecting items of evidence. Three spent shell casings were found on the floor on the customer side of the counter. It appeared to John Calvin that the killer stood on the customer side of the counter when he shot Alex Moyer, who was standing behind the counter.

While the coroner and his assistant were removing the body, John stood by watching. "Bill, something's wrong here," he remarked to Detective McGowen. "Look here." He pointed to a small safe behind and underneath the counter and bolted to the floor. The safe door was open; inside were proof sets of silver dollars, a white envelope and a large brown billfold. The flap on the envelope was open, and numerous bills could be seen inside. "It don't appear to be a robbery," he said.

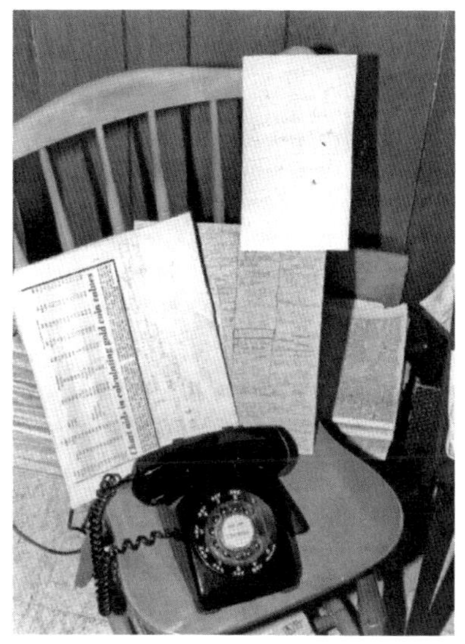

Telephone and gold coin value charts on a chair inside the coin shop. *Courtesy of Visalia Police Department.*

"But John," McGowen responded while standing on the customer side of the counter, "from this side you can't see the safe. Maybe the killer didn't know the safe was there."

"Yeah, but what about these coins in here?" John nodded toward numerous silver coins in small displays on a shelf inside the counter and visible through the glass countertop. "To get these he's gotta break the glass or come around on this side. There's no sign of a struggle—it looks like he was taken by surprise. Could've been a grudge of some kind."

At the far end of the counter near a telephone, McGowen found a piece of paper with the notations "DAVID-FRESNO" and some figures—"10-20'S, 10-5'S, 20-K"—listed in a row. He placed his initials and the date on the upper corner of the paper and gave it to the identification officer to place in evidence. He then began inspecting the drawers built into the counter just under the glass counter display case. McGowen noted that one drawer was about one-quarter open and, upon examining it, exclaimed, "John, look here!" Lying inside the drawer was a fully loaded .22-caliber Browning automatic pistol. "His feet were here," said McGowen, pointing just in front of the drawer. "He could've been going for the gun. This drawer was partially opened."

"He maybe went for it when he saw the killer's gun but got plugged before he could get the drawer open," Calvin surmised.

"It looks like he was taken by surprise, but if it was a robbery the killer panicked when he fired and left without taking anything," McGowen responded. "Unless he took something that was already on the counter top and didn't bother with anything else."

Across the room on the large table, an electric coffee maker was plugged in, and there was a small residue at the bottom of the glass coffeepot. What appeared to be coffee stains were on the floor near the table. A half-full cup of coffee was found on the desk at the end of the counter roughly five feet from the body. "The poor bastard didn't even get to finish his coffee," lamented John.

The door to the small bathroom was locked, and the key, on a key ring with other keys, was in the lock. There was another set of keys lying on the table. McGowen checked the burglar alarm and found it to be operative but turned off.

It was early afternoon as the two homicide detectives and the identification officer were taking final measurements when a man appeared at the doorway of the coin shop. "Excuse me," he called to the policemen, "I just heard about the murder and might have some information for you." Calvin went outside to question him.

"My name's Lester Morris and this is my office," he said, gesturing to a small office in the same building and immediately adjacent to the coin shop. "I was working yesterday and thought there was something unusual over there." He went on to explain that he knew Alex Moyer only by sight since he had been renting the office next to the coin shop for only some nine months. Morris said he would normally come to the office on Saturday mornings to do his paperwork and would see Moyer in his shop. They would wave but otherwise had no particular contact. Lester often brought his two young children with him on Saturday mornings to sweep the area in front of the office and generally clean up the parking lot. During these times, Moyer always came to the front door of his shop and spoke a few words to the children. Other than this, however, Moyer would usually remain inside the coin shop with the door locked, opening it only to allow a customer inside.

Lester Morris continued, noting that the previous day, Saturday, he arrived at his office at 11:30 a.m. He noticed Moyer's blue Cadillac parked in front of the building and the lights on inside the shop but did not see Mr. Moyer. He said that, upon thinking back on that morning, he recalled two things that were somewhat unusual. First, Moyer's Cadillac was not parked in the spot where it was normally parked, and second, Moyer failed to come to the door and speak to the children as they cleaned up the parking lot. Morris stayed at his office until 3:30 p.m. that afternoon.

On two occasions, Lester observed vehicles drive up to the front of the coin shop; the drivers walked to the front door and knocked, only to have the door unanswered. The first person got back into his car, a red Pacer, and drove away. The second person drove up in a Volkswagen, and after his knock went unanswered, he came to Lester's office and asked him if he had seen Mr. Moyer. Upon being told by Lester that he had not seen the coin shop owner, the man, described as tall and in his sixties, got into the Volkswagen and drove away.

When Lester Morris left that afternoon, the blue Cadillac was in the same location, and the shop lights were still on. He further explained that during the day, there were no noises or sounds coming from the coin shop.

Calvin recorded the statement in a small spiral notebook, and like all detectives, he had his own version of shorthand using a combination of abbreviations and symbols which only the author could decipher. He liked to recount a murder case several years before when a "hotshot Hollywood lawyer" was representing the accused and questioned John's report of what a witness had told him. After a lengthy discovery motion in court, the defense was given the right to inspect all notes taken by the police. John was ordered to produce his notes to the defense attorney. However, as he explained it, "That lawyer bastard couldn't make heads or tails from 'em." To John, the designation "bastard" applied to those he liked, pitied or hated.

As Calvin and McGowen drove back to the station, their discussion centered on when the killing took place, the consensus being that it must have occurred before 11:30 a.m. on Saturday, the time when Lester Morris arrived at his office. As events developed, the time of Alex Moyer's death would be the most compelling issue in convicting his killer.

THE VICTIM'S FAMILY

Visalia being a typical small town in the 1970s and 1980s, it had a relatively low crime rate. The usual drug and alcohol violations, shoplifting, occasional burglaries and the normal array of barroom fights composed the bulk of the police work. A murder, however, was big news, and the one newspaper in town, the *Visalia Times-Delta*, could be expected to make it a headline story.

John Calvin's thoughts ran to an unsolved murder case from September 1975 in which an instructor at the local community college had been shot and killed by an intruder in his home. The Moyer killing had all the same earmarks—no visible leads, no witnesses to the shooting and, on the surface at least, no clues to the identity of the killer. John set the wheels in motion to begin the investigation. He assigned McGowen to contact all surrounding homes and businesses to determine if anyone had seen or heard anything out of the ordinary. As any experienced investigator knew, even the slightest unusual act could lead to a possible solution.

John took upon himself the unhappy task of contacting and informing the victim's family. Taped on the inside of the glass front door was a small piece of paper. On the paper were two telephone numbers that could be contacted in case of emergency. One was for a Frank Moyer Jr. in Exeter, a small town some twelve miles east of Visalia. The other was for a Frank Moyer Sr., with a telephone number that Calvin recognized as having an area code number from the central coast. He concluded that this was the family contact that he had to make. He also wanted to have a family member with him to more thoroughly inventory the coin shop in search of possible leads.

As the detective in charge, Calvin had the task of preparing a news release. In addition to Visalia's one newspaper, there were newspapers of major circulation in the nearby cities of Tulare and Porterville. Fresno's paper, the *Fresno Bee*, was the Central Valley's largest newspaper, and it carried major crime stories from the Visalia area. Besides newspaper coverage, the news media in the Central Valley included radio stations in Visalia and Fresno, as well as in many of the smaller towns. Television stations in Visalia, Fresno and Bakersfield likewise covered major crime stories from the Visalia area.

In preparing his news release, he was careful to include only the victim's name, the time and location of the discovery of the murder and the names of the police personnel working the case. The reason for releasing only a small amount of information was to filter out those persons who might come forward with bogus information or even confessions. Should their statements not comport with the true physical facts, they could be discounted as cranks or merely mistaken. This is particularly important when an accomplice might come forward and give information to the police. If the information can be verified through the facts known only by the police, his or her credibility can be quickly determined.

"Is Mr. Frank Moyer Sr. available?" John said to the woman who answered the telephone.

She responded by saying, "Yes he is, who is calling please?" When John identified himself as calling from the Visalia Police Department, there was a pause, and then the woman said, "One moment please." John hated these moments of police work more than any others—the breaking of tragic news to a victim's family. He often wondered how he would react upon being informed of the death or serious injury of a loved one. This moment was particularly awkward because he had to communicate by telephone, as the Moyers lived in Santa Barbara, some 150 miles west of Visalia.

"This is Frank Moyer," said the voice of an apparently older man.

John again identified himself and asked if he was the father of the Frank Moyer who operated a stamp and coin shop in Visalia. When informed that he was, John began with, "Mr. Moyer I have some bad news for you." Then a pause. "Your son has been shot."

"Oh my God, is he dead?" asked the man.

"I'm sorry he is sir."

Following a few awkward moments while the tragic news took hold, John was then told by Mr. Moyer that he and his wife would be leaving from Santa Barbara to Visalia immediately. The drive was approximately a four-hour journey, and they expected to arrive just before midnight. Arrangements were made to meet at the police station at 8:00 a.m. Monday morning.

It was 9:30 p.m. when John told the dispatcher that he was going home. On the way, he stopped at the corner grocery to purchase some Alka-Seltzer for his churning stomach.

The couple that met with Detective John Calvin in his office Monday morning were noticeably tired and haggard looking. Mr. Moyer was a tall, white-haired man in his late seventies. Although he was of fair complexion, he gave the appearance of one who spent considerable time out of doors. Standing ramrod straight, lean of build and dressed in slacks and a knit golfing shirt, he looked the part of a physically active senior citizen. His wife, whom he introduced as "Louise Moyer, Alex's stepmother," was a well-groomed, tastefully dressed, attractive lady who appeared about the same age as her husband. Both were the type of people one liked and felt comfortable with soon after becoming acquainted.

It soon became apparent that Louise Moyer was the calmer of the two, as her husband seemed to still be in a state of shock. "Is there anybody that you know of who may have had any arguments or business disputes with your son?" asked John.

"Not that I'm aware of. Alex—everyone called him Alex, his middle name is Alexander—never mentioned any business problems or anything like that," responded Frank Moyer. "He had no partners or employees. Oh, he did hire a college kid named David to do some odd jobs for him on occasion and there was a fella who helped him build some shelves and cabinets. What was his name Louise, you know that fella who was always so nervous?"

"That was a man named Lonnie," she answered. "He was not quite right mentally, he had emotional problems but he was extremely nice and polite. He and Alex seemed to get along well."

"That was it," said Mr. Moyer, "Lonnie Pullman was his name."

"What about your son's home life, was he married or separated?" John asked.

"No," answered his father. "He never did marry, was always something of a loner."

"What about any lady friends that you know of?" inquired John.

"He never brought any to our house when he would visit, nor did he ever introduce us to any here in Visalia. I don't remember him ever mentioning any women that he was seeing, but you see Alex never talked much about himself, he was always quite independent," explained Louise Moyer.

"So what you're tellin' me is that you don't know of any enemies he had, or any jealous girlfriends, or anybody else who might've done this."

"Not that I can think of," responded Frank Moyer. "I racked my brain about this all night and can think of no one. I can't even think of any reason. It seems so senseless."

"Alex was well liked by everyone," added Louise. "He was always quiet, never offended anyone, there just appears no reason why this would happen."

"Well, I can tell you there's a lot of weirdos out there," said John in his own blunt manner. They made plans to inventory the coin shop together on Tuesday, for as John indicated, there might have been something in the shop that the killer was after. That Monday, the Moyers were making funeral arrangements and awaiting the arrival of Frank Moyer Sr.'s daughter (sister to the victim) and her family from Kansas.

Just before they left the police station that morning, Detective McGowen showed them the piece of paper he had found in the shop with the handwritten notation "DAVID-FRESNO," along with some figures. When asked if he recognized the writing, Frank Moyer responded, "That's Alex's writing. He always printed and used capital letters." He told the detectives that he was familiar with gold and silver coins, as he often bought and sold such coins himself, and explained that the figures on the note appeared to be an order for U.S. gold coins and Kuggarands.

The two detectives met the Moyers at the coin shop Tuesday morning and spent most of the day conducting an inventory of items found in the shop. They took note of all the items of memorabilia. There were silver coins in display cases on a shelf inside the counter. They also found several hundred dollars' worth of silver coins neatly packed in small cardboard boxes located

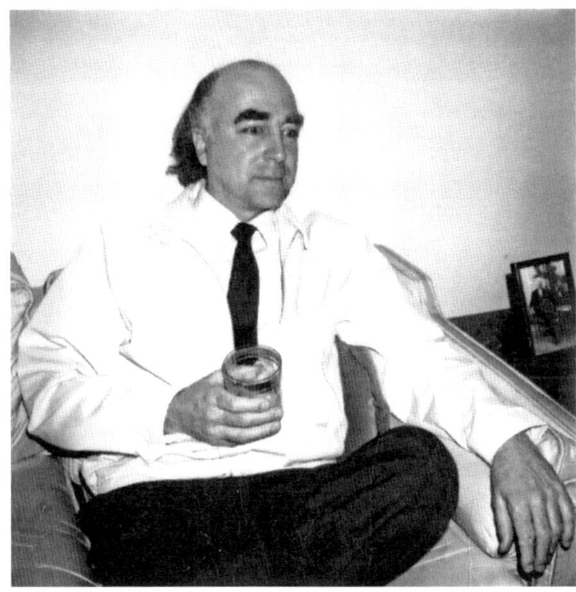

Alex Moyer at Christmas 1978. It was his last. *Courtesy of Frank Moyer Sr.*

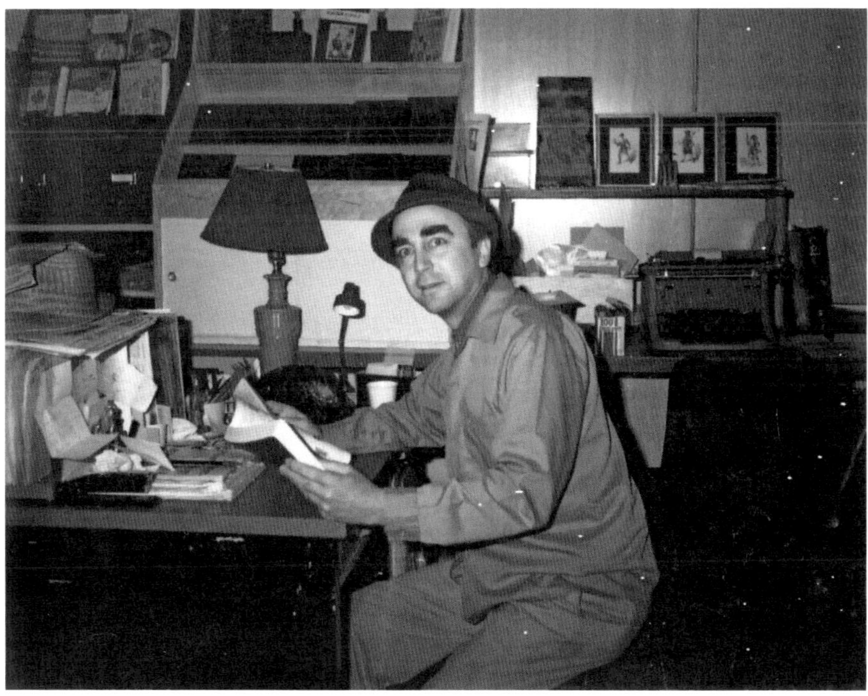

Alex Moyer at his first coin shop, 1972. *Courtesy of Frank Moyer Sr.*

in a briefcase that had been pushed under the counter area and was not visible from the customer side of the counter.

Upon further search, two gold coins were found lying loose in the safe. Frank Moyer identified them as a five-dollar coin and a twenty-dollar gold coin known as a Krugerrand. "Detective, this is rather strange," exclaimed Mr. Moyer. "From what I understand about the business Alex was doing, he should have many more gold coins. The price for gold has been fluctuating wildly lately and I would expect he would have had a much larger inventory than just two coins." This statement turned out to be crucial to solving the case.

THE MOYER AUTOPSY

Bill McGowen always became slightly nauseated by the antiseptic smell present in hospitals and doctors' offices. The nausea became stronger on those occasions when he attended an autopsy, and the autopsy in this case was no exception. The strong and pungent odors of ethyl alcohol, disinfectants and other chemical mixtures when combined with the odor of body gases, waste, undigested food and exposed human organs were enough to cause him to become faint. The husky six-footer had embarrassingly fainted when he had a blood test to obtain his marriage license. That had been sixteen years ago, but the apprehension of needles and dislike of doctors' offices remained.

John played on McGowen's discomfort in these situations. He delighted in innocently calling McGowen's attention to certain parts of the anatomy. "Look at this bullet hole through the heart, Bill. Stand over here so you can see it better," enthused John, winking at Dr. John Morrison, the pathologist.

Dr. Morrison, aware of McGowen's squeamish nature, played the role along with Calvin. "Here Bill, hold this back," he said to McGowen, referring to a portion of the deceased's chest cavity, "I have to remove the lung for examination."

"Come on, you big pussy," urged Calvin. "The poor bastard won't feel a thing."

"I was doing okay until you sawed open the chest," explained McGowen. "That gets me every time."

John Morrison was a stocky thirty-nine-year-old who had been practicing medicine for five years. He and his two partners contracted with Tulare

County on a yearly basis to do all the forensic pathology. Well liked by homicide detectives and prosecutors, Morrison was an excellent witness in court. With his close-cropped hair and horn-rimmed glasses, he exuded a mature demeanor that belied his years. Having studied ballistics and firearms extensively and attended many seminars on the subject, he was a highly qualified ballistics expert. In addition, he was an avid firearm collector. This made him all the more effective as a prosecution witness since he could not only testify to the fatal injuries received by a gunshot homicide victim, but he could often explain the ballistics and weapon types and capabilities involved as well.

The autopsy revealed the victim, Frank Alexander Moyer Jr., as being five feet, eight inches in height, weighing approximately 165 pounds and appearing to be physically fit for his age of forty-nine years. The shirt worn by the victim was blood soaked in the upper chest and back area. Dr. Morrison found five gunshot wounds in the victim's body. The first one observed was through the left forearm, shattering the bone. This shot passed through and appeared to have struck the left chest area, where there was noted a large bruise. "This round probably went through the forearm and struck him in the chest," explained Morrison, "but because it went through the bone in the forearm it lost enough force that it didn't penetrate his chest. I can't find this round, it's probably at the scene."

"We found a twenty-two caliber slug under the body," said George Jewett, a police identification technician who was also in attendance. "That could be it."

"That's probably it 'cause a twenty-two would lose most of its force after passing through this bone," replied Morrison. After bending the left forearm in front of the victim's chest in the position the arm was at the time of the shooting, he then placed a thin metal rod through the bullet hole in the arm depicting the flight path of the bullet. Jewett then photographed the victim.

"This is a defensive wound," said Morrison, referring to the type of wound known in homicide cases as one received by a person while trying to ward off or evade an attack. The defensive wound is oftentimes the result of a natural human reaction where the victim will cover up his chest, face or head area when his instincts tell him that an assailant is going to strike or shoot him in that area.

The second shot entered from the front of the victim in the chest area just slightly to the left of center, penetrating into and recovered from the left lung. It was not necessarily fatal. Dr. Morrison then found three gunshot wounds that entered the back of the deceased just to the left of the midline of the back. These three shots entered within inches of one another, and each penetrated the left lung. One was recovered in the liver, the other two penetrated the heart and were recovered in the sternum. Any of these alone could have caused death. All of the spent slugs were .22-caliber long rifle variety.

In addition to the gunshot wounds, Dr. Morrison examined and documented a laceration at the point of the chin and multiple lacerations on the outside and inside of the right upper lip. It was Morrison's opinion, as he stated in his notes taken while conducting the autopsy, that the chin injury was "most consistent with a fall" and the lip injury was "most consistent with a blow." Neither of these injuries were fatal.

"The shot to the forearm was probably the first, then the second shot to the chest area knocked him down," said Morrison. "Then the dirty son of a bitch pumped them other rounds into his back while he was on the floor," added Calvin. This was agreed to by Morrison. Because of the closeness in the pattern of the shots entering the back, it was evident that the victim was stationary when they were fired.

"You know, those cuts on the lip and chin could've come from hitting those shelves behind the counter when he fell," McGowen said. "There was only about three feet between the counter and the shelves, if he spun around at all he'd have bumped into those shelves."

"Yeah, he was on his stomach so his chin must've struck the floor," added Jewett.

The final anatomic diagnosis read: "Death due to multiple gunshot wounds and associated visceral injuries." A laboratory analysis of the blood revealed that Mr. Moyer had no alcohol or drugs in his system at the time of death.

WITNESSES

Dennis Gimlin was at his place of employment, Early California Foods in Exeter, on Monday, October 8, 1979. He operated a forklift loading and unloading large barrels of olives. Early California Foods processed, canned and distributed food products. The Exeter plant dealt exclusively in olives, as it was located in the heart of one of the major olive-producing areas in the San Joaquin Valley. The plant was on Highway 65, a major thoroughfare between Porterville in the southern part of the county and Highway 198.

Persons traveling to Visalia from Porterville, Exeter or anywhere in between would normally take Highway 65 north to Highway 198 and then travel some twelve miles west to the Visalia city limits. The loading yard where Dennis Gimlin worked fronted on Highway 65 and was visible to motorists both north- and southbound. The month of October was the midst of the harvest season for olives, and the plant was operating an average of ten hours a day, six days a week.

Dennis was on a break at about 3:15 p.m. that Monday afternoon when his wife telephoned the office and asked to speak to him. She had just received the *Visalia Times-Delta* edition for that Monday that headlined the Moyer murder on the front page. Since her husband was a friend of Mr. Moyer's, she called to inform him of the tragic news.

"When did it happen?" he asked her. "I just saw him drive by the plant Saturday morning."

"The paper says that it probably happened on Saturday but he wasn't found until Sunday morning," she responded.

"He drove by and waved at me like he always does, but I remember thinking that evening that I didn't see him drive back. Do they know who did it?" he asked. She told him that the article indicated there were no suspects and the police were investigating.

"Maybe I better tell the police when I saw him, it might help," he said, unaware then just how important an establishment of Alex Moyer's activities on Saturday morning would turn out to be. "Remind me tonight to call them when I get home, okay?"

That evening, John Calvin met with Dennis at the Gimlin apartment. He related to John that he had known Moyer for about fifteen years, having first met him while a student in high school when he became an avid stamp collector. He had remained a steady customer over the years because, as Dennis explained, "I'm a stamp collecting freak." He had no interest in the coins or gold and silver and knew little of Moyer's business or customers in that regard, except it was his understanding that in the past few months the gold business had been quite active. Dennis estimated that he would visit the shop several times a month to buy, sell or trade stamps with Moyer.

He then went on to tell Calvin that Alex Moyer would always honk and wave to him as he drove past the olive yard and that he had done so that Saturday morning but did not remember him doing so that afternoon. When Calvin asked what time Saturday morning Moyer drove past, Dennis responded, "It was between nine-thirty and ten." This time would prove vital, as things turned out.

The telephones at the Visalia Police Department were busy that Monday with persons calling about the Moyer murder. Unlike a large metropolitan area, where such occurrences are taken as routine, in the year 1979 Visalia still had the typical small-town mentality where such events, being few and far between, are the subject of nearly every conversation. The murder of Alex Moyer would have enlivened the discussions in barbershops, grocery store checkout lines, among people in small cafés where local merchants and farmers would gather for breakfast and lunch and nearly anywhere in town where the news topics of the day would be discussed. These discussions often ended with the participants agreeing in a common belief that the death penalty should be strictly enforced and bewilderment why "the liberal judges and do-gooders keep turning killers and rapists and thieves loose." Most of these telephone calls to the police were from persons who knew Moyer and frequented his shop. Either Calvin or McGowen talked to each caller, taking down all information that could possibly lead to the identity of the killer.

One of these callers identified himself as David Dye. Based on what he was told, McGowen asked Dye to come to the police station for an interview. He arrived just before noon. David Dye was a tall, blond-haired young man who gave his age as twenty-five years. He wore a mustache and beard, and his deep tan gave the appearance of someone who spent much of his time out of doors. This physical appearance, along with his mild mannerisms, gave McGowen the image of someone who might be found in a forest studying plant life.

David told McGowen that he was a friend and occasional employee of Alex Moyer. He had originally met Mr. Moyer some ten years before and, like Dennis Gimlin, was an avid stamp collector often frequenting the stamp and coin shop. When Alex Moyer moved his shop to the Murray Street location some years before, David would assist Moyer in cataloguing stamps, taking stamp orders over the phone and assisting in appraising stamps. For these efforts, he would be paid a small amount, which he usually took in the form of credit toward the purchase of stamps. In the summer and fall of 1978, he worked several afternoons a week and a few hours on Saturday mornings. On three occasions, he ran the shop for a few days at a time when Mr. Moyer was out of town. During this time in 1978, he was given a key to the shop. He told McGowen, however, that he returned the key in December when he went to Fresno to attend college for the spring semester in 1979.

McGowen asked about the locking device on the shop door. "He used a deadbolt lock and always kept it locked," explained Dye. "Alex was super cautious and wouldn't let anyone in the shop unless he knew who they were. He would always lock the door after he let someone in." When asked where the key was kept, David explained that Moyer had one key on his key chain with his car and house keys and another key that was left in the lock while he was in the shop. However, he would take this second key with him whenever he left the shop.

David also explained that Moyer would take all valuable gold and silver items and cash with him when he closed the shop and would bring them back with him on the next business day. "He had a brown satchel that looked something like a small suitcase, sort of like a doctor's bag. He was a super cautious person. He even had wrought iron bars put on the windows of his house." In response to the detective's question about Moyer's friends and acquaintances, David responded, "He was a very private person, he had lots of friends who visited the store but none of them seemed like real close friends. Everyone liked Alex and he was always friendly and talkative. He had a group of friends that played bridge in the shop a couple of nights a week a year or so ago. I can't think of anyone off hand who would have killed him. He really had no enemies that I knew of."

David told McGowen that the last time he was in the shop was the previous Tuesday afternoon, when he stopped in to look over new stamp arrivals. He did, however, notice something unusual on Saturday evening. At about 6:00 p.m., he was in a small convenience store located at the corner of Murray Street and Giddings Avenue one short block from the coin shop. He explained that as he left the store, he glanced toward the coin shop and saw lights on and Moyer's blue Cadillac parked in front. Thinking it was unusual for Mr. Moyer to still be at the shop this late, he debated whether to go by, but since he was on foot, he decided against it. As he explained, "I figured he would be playing cards or talking to some friends." Then, almost as an afterthought, he added, "I wish I'd gone by."

Summer weather usually arrives in the San Joaquin Valley the first week of June. The pleasant weather of March, April and May, accompanied by crystal-clear skies dotted with puffy white clouds, ever so welcome after the cold and foggy winter months, finally gives way to the onset of the hot weather. Temperatures begin to soar from the daytime spring highs in the seventies and mid-eighties up to the nineties and occasionally giving a foretaste of the one-hundred-degree weather typical of the Valley in July and August. This hot weather, when accompanied by a sufficient amount of water, is a prime reason why the San Joaquin Valley is the nation's leading agricultural area.

The hot days and warm nights of summer gradually fade away in the month of September. Nights become cool, and daytime highs drop to the mid-eighties and below. Many trees and shrubs begin to lose their foliage in late September, and by the end of October and early November, the fruit groves and residential lawns are covered by fallen leaves.

The smallish, gray-haired man was concerned about his lawn, in which he took great pride. He had seeded it with winter rye grass a few years before in order to maintain a green lawn during the autumn and into the winter months. The falling leaves from the many trees along the sidewalk in front of his house would cover the lawn area and prevent the necessary sunlight from getting through. This problem kept him busy raking fallen leaves several times a week at this time of year. He had allowed a few days to go by without removing the leaves, and for one who was fussy about the appearance of his lawn, it was time to rake them again.

The man, dressed in slacks, a flowered shirt, white socks and canvas sneakers and topped by a wide-brimmed straw hat, looked the part of a retired bank president turned weekend gardener as he raked up the fallen leaves and placed them into trash barrels.

This Monday morning, his wife was at her weekly hairdresser appointment, and he planned on attending to a few gardening chores before going to the Visalia Stamp and Coin Shop to purchase some gold coins. He was still in the yard at 11:30 a.m. that morning when his wife returned. Claire Lawson excitedly called to her husband as she turned into the driveway, "Henry, Henry did you hear the news?"

The man, not one to become moved by his wife's frequent outbursts of nervous excitement, answered without stopping his raking, "No, I haven't."

"Henry, Henry!" she exclaimed as she exited the car. "What's your stamp dealer's name? You know the one who has the shop across from the Oaks baseball park."

"His name is Alex Moyer, why?"

"Henry, he's been murdered—right in his shop!" she said. The man seemed stunned and stared at her in disbelief. "The girls in the beauty shop told me. They found him yesterday in his shop, he'd been shot. A neighbor found him on the floor."

"A neighbor? You mean at his house?" he asked puzzled.

"No, no, a neighbor next door to the shop," she explained. "The police don't know who did it."

Still in a state of disbelief, Henry Lawson sat down on the steps of the front porch. "Claire," he murmured, "I just saw him Friday evening. When did it happen?"

"I heard that the police think it happened on Saturday because his car was seen there then and it was still there on Sunday when they found him," she answered.

"He told me Friday that he had an appointment to sell all of his gold and silver to a man on Saturday morning," he muttered as he tried to recall his last contact with Alex Moyer.

"Henry you better tell the police what you know, it could be important," she responded.

"I'll do that right now. I'm going to call the police station," he said as he entered the house. Lawson telephoned the Visalia Police Department, told the desk officer that he may have some information on the Alex Moyer murder and asked to speak to the detective handling the case. He was transferred to John Calvin's extension. Arrangements were made to meet with Calvin at the police station that afternoon.

Henry Lawson was a transplanted midwesterner. A friendly and personable man in his sixties, he spent most of his working career in the radio broadcasting business. Born and raised in Kansas City, Missouri, he left college after two years to accept a job with a small radio station in southern Illinois. After a few years working as an assistant program director, writer and promoter, he began announcing by doing the news and weather, station breaks and commercials. When World War II broke out, he went into the navy, returning in 1945 to the same job.

During the 1950s, he was involved with a group of investors that purchased a radio station in Kansas. He continued buying and selling interests in radio stations in the Midwest until he came to Visalia in the early 1970s to "finally get away from the blizzards and tornadoes." He acquired a majority interest in a Visalia radio station that he sold in 1977 for a substantial profit. Retired, he and his wife lived a quiet life in a modest yet established Visalia neighborhood, occasionally traveling to Kansas to visit their daughter and her family.

The man John Calvin met at his office that afternoon was dressed in a conservative business suit, white shirt and tie. Henry Lawson had not yet adapted to the less formal atmosphere of California. To him, his appointment with Detective Calvin was in the nature of a business meeting despite the unpleasant subject matter. The two men introduced themselves, shook hands and walked to John's small office. "How about some coffee?" John asked.

"No thanks," responded Lawson. "I can't drink it after lunchtime because it'll keep me awake all night."

Henry Lawson then explained that he had known Alex Moyer for about five years, having met him when he purchased some stamps for his grandson's collection. After that purchase, he would go to the shop on occasion to look for particular stamps for the grandson, who lived in Kansas. After retiring, he frequented the shop more often, estimating that he would visit with Mr. Moyer "maybe an average of a few hours every two weeks or so. We were not close friends, but we used to talk with each other a lot," he explained. "Sometimes I would stop in and give him a market letter that I had. He was interested in the stock market."

After being told by Lawson that he had seen the victim on October 3, the Wednesday before the murder, and again on Friday, October 5, John asked, "Okay, tell me why you went there on Wednesday."

Henry went on to explain;

> *Well I belong to the Rotary Club here in Visalia; and that Wednesday at the Rotary meeting a friend of mine who is a jeweler in town remarked to me that he needed some gold coins, I don't know, to set in a bracelet or something. But he wanted two or three gold coins. He said "do you happen to know anybody that has any for sale?" I said, "Well, the only person I could think of would be Mr. Moyer who usually had a number of gold coins."*
>
> *And this friend of mine happens to be in a wheel chair, he can't get around very well. And I said, "I only live a couple of blocks from Mr. Moyer's shop. I live on Todd Drive, and I go past there on the way home from Rotary." And I said "I'd stop by and ask Mr. Moyer if he had any. If he does I'll either have him call you or, perhaps, he'll let me take them over to you to look at them." And so I stopped by that afternoon into Mr. Moyer's shop. That was the only reason for dropping in.*

"Let me ask you this," John interrupted, "what time was it you dropped in?"

"Rotary wasn't out until about a quarter of two. And I think I stopped by Dean Witter after that. I would guess it was between three-thirty and five." Lawson went on to explain that when he arrived at the shop, "Moyer had the door locked as he usually did, and he saw me at the door and he opened it."

"Did he keep the door locked?" John interrupted again.

"Oh yes, he has a glass door and it was a double-keyed lock. You could put the key in from inside or outside the store." John questioned where

Moyer kept the key. "When I usually saw it, it was hanging on the inside of the door."

> *Okay, as I was saying, I contacted Mr. Moyer and told him of this friend of mine that would like to buy two or three gold coins and I promised to check with him and asked if he had them. He said, "Yes, I have the coins." But I wasn't able to obtain them because he informed me, he said, "Henry I had a call from Fresno this week." And he said that "the man wants to buy all of my gold coins, and he's supposed to come down on Friday and pick them up." He said, "if you drop back on Friday afternoon, if he doesn't pick them up, then you can have the coins for your friend, or have him get in touch with me." And he said, "but I've given my word, and I can't let you have the coins now because the party who called said he wanted all of my gold coins."*

Henry Lawson then went on to explain that he went back on Friday afternoon at about four o'clock. He said, "I walked in and asked about the coins. Mr. Moyer stated that the man who was purchasing his coins had called and said he was not able to make it on Friday, and he was coming down on Saturday morning to pick them up. Mr. Moyer said, 'I don't want to lose this sale because he's also told me now that he wants to buy all of the silver that I have on hand.' That was it. The next thing I know Mr. Moyer was killed."

"Was that the last time you saw him, that Friday afternoon?" asked John.

"Yes, I was going to go to his store this afternoon and see if he had any coins left. My wife heard about it at her beauty shop appointment and told me. That's when I called the police department." Lawson was unable to supply anything further in identifying the customer from Fresno other than the fact that he had told Alex Moyer that he had sold all of his stock and wanted to invest his money in gold.

"Do you have any suspects?" asked Henry.

"We're working on it. We're taking statements from anyone who knew him," John responded. "Do you know any other persons who were there that Friday?"

"There was a fella from Sanger who I've met before," Henry answered. "He and Alex would usually talk bridge. They were discussing some book on bridge when I arrived Friday and then the gentleman left. I don't know his name but he's about forty-five years old with short gray hair and real tall—well over six feet."

As they concluded their conversation, John walked with Mr. Lawson to the lobby. "You know this is really a tragic thing," he said. "Like I say, we were good friends. He was a fine and honest person. It's really a shame; you can count on me if you need me in court." How prophetic those words were.

The week following the homicide was a hectic one for both Calvin and McGowen but produced no significant leads. Many customers or friends of Alex Moyer contacted the police department and generally related that they either purchased or sold gold and/or silver in transactions with him. The upshot of all these conversations was that Alex Moyer was dealing heavily in gold and silver during the months before his murder. Indeed, the precious metals market, especially gold, was fluctuating wildly during the summer and fall of 1979, and dealers and investors were trading in great volume and with great frequency. It was beginning to appear to the detectives that the murder was somehow connected with the gold and silver sales and purchases.

On Thursday following the murder, Frank Moyer brought several canceled checks and other records belonging to his son to the police department. Calvin and McGowen spent the majority of the afternoon trying to decipher the records. As would be later verified after talking to many gold and silver dealers, they became aware that records of such transactions often were either not kept or were kept in a sloppy fashion. Some of the notations in the records showed $1,501.50 from "Jerry," $6,720 purchased from "Cogel" and $4,812.50 from "Harris Metal." No address or further information was indicated. John assigned McGowen to follow up on the canceled checks by contacting the payees named on the checks.

A Change Is Made

The long hours put into the investigation of the Moyer murder took its toll on John Calvin's physical condition. His ulcer pained him, and his blood pressure soared. As John himself said while puffing on an ever-present cigarette and guzzling black coffee, "My gut feels like a gawdamn bowlin' alley." However, it was an occurrence during the following week that so adversely affected his health that he had to be removed from his investigative duties and assigned to less stressful duties.

On June 6, 1979, exactly four months to the day before the Moyer homicide, a robbery-murder had occurred on the north side of Visalia. In the early morning hours of that day, Gilbert and Helen Vega were preparing to leave on vacation. They were part of a group that was to board a bus in the nearby town of Selma and travel to Reno, Nevada, for a five-day stay. Gilbert Vega, a furniture salesman, had been instrumental in organizing the trip and had, in fact, solicited some of his neighbors to join. It was this solicitation that alerted certain neighborhood youths to the fact that the Vegas would be leaving in the early morning hours that day and would be carrying a large amount of cash with which to gamble.

The area where the Vegas lived in north Visalia was economically lower middle class in nature but was known for sporadic incidents of violence. These incidents were generally associated with the North Visalia Community Center, a small park and building where teenage activities were sponsored by the city recreation department. After closing hours, the park was frequented by local youths engaging in drinking and drug activity, which often led to acts of violence. Within the first six months of 1979 alone, there had been two stabbings, one over a drug deal gone bad and another over ownership of a six-pack of beer; two reports of "shots fired"; and numerous fights. Because of these incidents, the city recreation department was seriously considering closing the facility.

Following a night of beer drinking and smoking marijuana at the park, two carloads of youths drove the block and a half to the short cul-de-sac street where the Vegas' house was located. The two cars drove past the Vegas as they were loading their suitcases into their vehicle. Both cars stopped at the end of the street and turned off their lights. A few minutes later, the Vegas got into their car, and Gilbert Vega drove away from the house. At this time, the youths, who had been awaiting the Vegas' departure, overtook the vehicle, one car swinging around in front of it and the other driving closely behind.

The three vehicles drove in this manner around the corner, whereupon the car in front suddenly stopped, forcing the Vega vehicle to come to a stop. At this time, the trailing car pulled alongside and stopped slightly behind the Vega vehicle, preventing it from moving.

Two occupants of the front vehicle ran to the passenger side of the Vega automobile, where Helen Vega was seated. Richard Sanchez and two companions exited the other car and ran to the driver, Gilbert Vega. Richard held a small handgun to Vega's head and demanded all of his money. Gilbert Vega complied and pulled his wallet from his back pocket. As he handed the wallet to Sanchez, the gun went off, firing a bullet into Vega's head and killing him instantly. All the assailants then fled the scene.

John Calvin had received information from a confidential informant as to the identity of the persons involved. Mrs. Vega was shown a series of mug shots from which she picked out the shooter, Richard Sanchez, and the two persons who had approached her side of the car. The three were arrested and charged with murder and an allegation that it occurred during the commission of a robbery, thus invoking the death penalty. After many delays, the preliminary hearing was finally scheduled to begin on Monday, October 15.

The defense's contention was misidentification by Helen Vega, and the main thrust was that Calvin had acted improperly by conducting a "suggestive and prejudicial photographic show-up in violation of the defendants' constitutional right to due process of law." Calvin's response was simply put: "Those little punk bastards are guilty as hell. They can shove their rights right up their ass."

An attorney representing one of the defendants was Mark Hampton, a liberal, anti-police criminal defense attorney who had only recently left the Public Defender's Office. He was dogged and repetitious and often caustic and sarcastic in his questioning, producing anger from witnesses and boredom among court personnel. He was particularly aggressive toward police officers as witnesses. The clash with John Calvin promised to be most interesting.

The deputy district attorney didn't call John as a witness until Tuesday morning. His questioning led John through the selection of various photographs from police mug books of Mexican American males in their late teens or early twenties, compiling them into three separate displays and presenting them to Mrs. Vega for possible identification. The displays, each containing six photographs, one of which was of a suspect, were brought to court, identified by Calvin and offered into evidence. This questioning took approximately twenty minutes; cross-examination by the three defense attorneys lasted one and a half days.

Like most veteran police officers, John Calvin was a calm and professional witness. However, the caustic and repetitious cross-examination by Mark Hampton, coupled with the intensity brought about by Calvin's high blood pressure, caused the veteran detective to lose his composure several times during Hampton's cross-examination.

Two days later, while reading the evening paper at his home, John experienced a sudden severe headache and numbness on his left side. The next thing he was aware of was his wife leaning over him and frantically calling his name. The doctor on duty in the hospital emergency room that evening said that John had experienced a light to moderate stroke and had him admitted over night for continual observation. The following day, John's doctor agreed with the diagnosis and ordered John to rest at home for two months, assume a less stressful assignment at work, stop drinking and smoking and cut out all coffee and salt from his diet.

When Lieutenant Buddy Hale, in charge of the detective unit, received the word about John Calvin, he faced a dilemma. The Moyer case required two investigators at this stage to conduct all the follow-up necessary. To produce the best results, it is axiomatic that contacting witnesses and pursuing leads be done as soon as possible following a crime. Memories tend to fade, and people are difficult to locate as time goes by. Bill McGowen had other cases assigned to him, as well as some necessary court appearances, and without another detective to assist him in the Moyer case, it would cause difficulties in his other cases. Also, as Hale well knew, with all the publicity that the Moyer case was receiving, it was imperative to assign an experienced investigator to replace Calvin and direct the investigation.

The only person available was Sergeant Bill Wittman, who was in charge of property crimes and narcotic investigations. It appeared to Hale that Wittman would be the logical choice and made the assignment; however, Wittman was currently out of the county on vacation. In the meantime, McGowen would work alone attempting to sort out whatever leads he could.

As it stood, two weeks after the murder, the Moyer case had a new detective in charge of the investigation, although he was unaware of it at the time, and no suspects or concrete evidence. In the week before Sergeant Wittman was to return, McGowen worked alone attempting to contact all persons mentioned in Moyer's records as having recently done business with him. Many of the records were insufficient to even identify the party with whom Moyer had a transaction. Those records that could be traced to identifiable customers did not produce any significant information. Those customers all basically indicated that Alex Moyer was a friendly and nice guy, very cautious with whom he did business, had no known enemies and, like most other gold and silver dealers in 1979, was doing a considerable amount of business.

One of the customers contacted was Fred Sciacca, a local CPA who, on the Tuesday before the homicide, brought a large quantity of quarters to the shop to trade in. The reason McGowen contacted Mr. Sciacca was because of a canceled check found in Moyer's recently arrived bank statement. The check was made out to Fred Sciacca on October 2, 1979, in the amount of $2,350. McGowen's report of the interview with Sciacca contained one sentence that would eventually prove to be extremely important: "Mr. Sciacca said the deceased wanted to pay him in gold coin but Sciacca wanted cash." The significance was not apparent to McGowen at the time because he had not yet read John Calvin's report of the interview with Henry Lawson in which Moyer, on Wednesday, the day after the purchase of the Sciacca silver, had refused to sell any gold coins to Lawson because of an order by someone from Fresno.

Although no one was aware of it at the time, a major issue arose as to what had occurred between the Sciacca transaction that Tuesday and the Lawson attempt to purchase gold coins that Wednesday. What had happened between these two events that caused Moyer to change his mind about selling gold coins? Had an order for gold coins occurred that Moyer wanted to honor?

When Sergeant Wittman returned to work on Monday, October 29, Lieutenant Hale was waiting for him. Never one to use words unnecessarily, Hale greeted Wittman with, "Bill, John's heart went bad. You're in charge of the Moyer homicide. McGowen's workin' with you."

"Good mornin' to you too, Buddy," replied Wittman. "It's great to be back."

Part II
THE FRESNO COIN DEALER MURDER

The Disappearance

On Thursday, August 2, 1979, some nine and a half weeks before the Moyer murder, Fresno coin dealer James Bibee failed to return home from work. It was not like him to arrive home later than 5:30 p.m. in the evening, and if he was going to be late, he would always call his wife, Nell, and let her know. Besides, this day was special: it was his seventy-second birthday. Nell Bibee had prepared his favorite dinner, and when he still had not arrived home by 6:00 p.m., she became quite concerned.

Her husband suffered from a mild heart condition, and even though the medication he was taking seemed to stabilize it and he had been in good health, one could never tell when it might flare up again unexpectedly. She puttered around nervously, checking the window periodically and expecting to see his brown 1964 Chevrolet Impala appear in the driveway. It was nearly 6:30 p.m. when she decided to call her husband's business associate, Tom Duffy.

In his late seventies, Tom Duffy ran a small secondhand store and antique business on Blackstone Avenue in Fresno. He and James Bibee had been friends for more than twenty-five years. Tom rented a small portion in the rear of his store to Bibee, who bought, sold and traded gold and silver coins and occasional works of art. Both men were retired, and these businesses served to supplement their incomes, as well as provide a place to get together with their cronies and discuss the topics of the day.

Nell called Tom Duffy at his home. He had no knowledge of her husband's whereabouts; however, he did recall overhearing him say something about "buying some coins from that Stone fella."

"I never did like him," Tom Duffy said. "Let me call to his house and see what's goin' on."

"Would you please, Tom," exclaimed an anxious Nell Bibee. "Let me know what you find out."

"I'll get back to ya, Nell, soon's I find somethin' out."

It was 7:15 p.m. that evening before Duffy was able to contact anyone at the Stone residence on Backer Street in Fresno. As he later explained to the Fresno Police Department, "I wasn't too nice to that Stone fella, I never liked him and never trusted him." Duffy was told by David Stone that James Bibee had arrived at the Stone residence at 5:00 p.m. that evening. They traded some coins, and Mr. Bibee left at approximately 6:00 p.m. When he left, David Stone told Duffy that he had assumed that Mr. Bibee was on his way home, although he never made any statement indicating that he was going home.

As promised, Tom Duffy relayed what he had learned to Nell Bibee. In the meantime, she had contacted three hospitals in town, and no one by the name of James Bibee had been admitted that evening. When she called the Fresno Police Department, she was told that there were no accident reports involving a James Bibee. They also told her that a missing person report could not be filed until the following day.

It had been between 9:00 a.m. and 9:30 a.m. that August morning when James Bibee prepared to leave his home. He carried the large cardboard box containing his coins and other valuables to his brown Impala and placed it into the trunk. Among the items in the cardboard box was a small metal box containing gold coins and several narrow containers such as might hold wafers or cookies. In these containers were silver coins. It was Bibee's custom to transport these items each day rather than leave them at Duffy's Antique Shop. After closing the trunk, he went back into the house and told Nell he was leaving for the shop.

She reminded him that she was preparing his favorite dinner that evening. It was the Bibees' custom that on her birthday they would dine out at a fancy restaurant and for his birthday she would prepare his favorite meal. One week before, they had dined out to celebrate her sixty-fourth birthday, and tonight, it was home-cooked fried chicken, mashed potatoes and gravy. Even though Nell restricted her husband's diet according to his doctor's orders, she allowed this one treat on his birthday. He kissed her goodbye and walked outside to his car. Nell Bibee never saw her husband again.

Bibee left his home on Boyd Street in Fresno and drove the two miles to Duffy's Antique Shop, parked his car, opened the trunk and carried the cardboard box inside to his small display space. As was his custom, Tom Duffy had arrived at the shop at nine o'clock sharp, bringing the morning edition of the *Fresno Bee* with him and starting the coffee brewing. He greeted his friend James Bibee with a "happy birthday" and made some comment about birthdays being good luck. He couldn't have been more wrong.

Tom Duffy and James Bibee had a morning ritual of starting their workday by drinking coffee and reading through the newspaper. This morning's newspaper contained reports of what was becoming all too common: armed robbery, assaults and other violent crimes. The two men discussed these and deplored the fact that such crimes were becoming so commonplace. They were particularly aware of the robbery and murder of the couple from Visalia, the town some forty-five miles to the south, as they were leaving on vacation. Tom had commented at the time, "You can't be safe anywhere anymore."

Bibee eagerly turned to the financial page to check on the current price of gold. He was aware that the precious metals market, and most notably the gold market, had been fluctuating wildly as of late and that a smart trader could make a lot of money by buying and selling at the right time.

Harold Kelley would often come by Duffy's Antique Shop to visit and discuss the day's events with his friends. The fifty-eight-year-old was retired and in poor health, suffering from a variety of ailments, most significant of which was emphysema and heart problems. Like his friend James Bibee, he also bought and sold items both as a hobby and to supplement his retirement income. Rather than coins, however, Kelley dealt mainly in small items such as vases, plates and jewelry.

It was just after 11:30 a.m. when Harold Kelley arrived at Duffy's. After saying hello to Tom Duffy, who was at the front of the shop, Kelley walked to the back to wish his friend James Bibee a happy birthday. As he approached, he saw that Bibee was engaged in a conversation with a young man he knew by the name of David Stone. He overheard Stone say that his father had recently passed away and left him a large quantity of gold and silver coins that he wanted to trade. The conversation ended shortly after Kelley approached, and the young man left the shop. Harold Kelley wished James Bibee a happy birthday.

Harold stayed at Duffy's shop that whole day, visiting with both Tom and James and any of their other friends who would drop by during the day. He had been at the shop for about an hour when he had a conversation with Bibee about a jade figurine that he had sold to Bibee a few weeks before. Bibee intended to resell it and was uncertain what price he should ask. Kelley suggested that he ask $2,100, as this would give him some bargaining room with a buyer and still allow him to make a reasonable profit. When Bibee agreed that this would be a good starting price, Kelley made a small price tag and, using tape, affixed it to the blue, felt-covered box containing the jade figurine. This small rectangular price tag measuring about one inch by one-half inch in size would ultimately prove to be an invaluable connection between two brutal murders.

During this discussion, the telephone rang. Tom Duffy answered it and called James over, indicating it was David Stone asking for him. Harold Kelley could overhear Bibee discussing a possible coin transaction and saying that he would come by after work. He then heard Bibee ask David Stone for directions to his house. After hanging up, James Bibee said, "I'm gonna have to go to David's house because he can't bring the gold coins and the silver dollars to the shop." Harold Kelley thought to himself that this sounded strange. In all these years, he had never known Bibee to do business anywhere except from Duffy's shop, and he had never known him to go to a customer's house.

It was between 4:00 p.m. and 4:30 p.m. that afternoon when James Bibee mentioned that he had to be on his way since he had stops to make before he went home. Harold Kelley helped him take his belongings out to the car. As he did every time he left Duffy's, Bibee opened the trunk of the brown Chevrolet Impala and placed the large cardboard box inside. Kelley carried the blue, felt-covered box with the newly attached price tag containing the jade figurine and placed it into the cardboard box that Bibee had set inside the trunk area. They exchanged goodbyes, and James Bibee drove away. Harold Kelley never saw his friend again.

DISAPPEARANCE TURNS TO HOMICIDE

James Bibee did not return home that night, and a nearly hysterical Nell Bibee met with officers at the Fresno Police Department at 8:00 a.m. the next morning. She gave them a list of all persons her husband might have been in contact with, including David Stone. From the police department, she was taken by friends to her doctor, where she was given a sedative to calm her nerves.

Fresno Police Department detective Gary Snow began the investigation into the disappearance of James Bibee by contacting Tom Duffy at the antique store. By this time, it was midmorning on Friday, August 3. "That fella was in the store talkin' to Jim yesterday," recalled Duffy, "He was always hangin' around, talked big—like he was some kinda big shot coin dealer. Ol' Jim was too nice to him. Me, I'da run him out long ago." Duffy told the detective about contacting Stone the night before and said he had called again that morning. The more the older man talked, the more it became apparent to Detective Snow that he was taking his best friend's disappearance extremely hard. He was pacing back and forth and occasionally having shortness of breath.

"Mr. Duffy you might be better off if you sat down," said Snow. "Tell me about your contact with this David Stone this morning." As Tom Duffy pulled up a chair, he explained that the first time he called the Stone house that morning, a woman answered and told him David Stone was not there. He then called back an hour later at 8:30 a.m. and talked to David Stone. "I told him I thought he knew somethin' about ol' Jim and that we were gonna call the police."

"Where else might he have gone?" asked Detective Snow.

"You might check with Les Normart. He owns Normart Furs over on Blackstone. He and Jim were good friends and he went over there a lot," answered Duffy.

Detective Snow contacted Les Normart that morning and was told that James Bibee did stop by his business at around 4:30 p.m. Thursday afternoon. They had a cup of coffee together, and Bibee went to the safe in the back of the store. Les Normart told the detective, "Jim Bibee was a life-long friend of my father and I've known him since I was a little kid. I let him use the safe to keep some of his coins and cash in, he had been doing this for over twenty years." Although he did not pay particular attention, Les Normart said that he seemed to remember that Mr. Bibee had removed only some money from the safe. "Then he made a remark about going to someone's house to buy some gold coins. In looking back on it, this was strange 'cause he did all of his business at Duffy's shop. I don't ever remember him going to a customer's house."

Detective Snow called the Stone residence twice that day and both times was told by a woman that David Stone was not at home. He detected a nervousness in the woman's voice when he identified himself and left his number with a request that Mr. Stone contact him.

No trace of James Bibee or his automobile was found that Friday. Saturday arrived and still there was no sign of what had become of the coin dealer. However, early that morning, a man who had been jogging reported to the police that he found a quantity of assorted coins strewn along a canal bank near the Stardust Motel on North Blackstone. The coins found were not rare and were valued in the neighborhood of $150. Later that Saturday, two more reports were received of persons finding assorted coins. These were located along residential streets some four to five blocks from the Stardust Motel. Significantly, a small, empty, oblong cardboard box that could hold twenty-five silver dollars was found with one group of coins. On the box was some printing that Tom Duffy identified as James Bibee's. Detective Snow was now certain that they were dealing with a kidnaping and robbery, as well as possibly a homicide.

While working some leads, Gary Snow received a call on his police radio informing him that a David Stone had called and left word that he could be contacted at his parents' house in Fresno at 4:00 p.m. At the appointed time, Snow drove to the home of Mr. and Mrs. Eston Stone, located in an area of upper middle-class homes on San Jose Street in Fresno. As he approached, he saw a young man standing on the lawn area next to the curb. The young man appeared to be in his early twenties, was of a pale-white complexion and had sandy blond hair. He appeared to be about five-foot-seven in height and somewhat overweight. Detective Snow got the immediate impression that the young man was not particularly physical in nature. He had a paunchy, soft, "couch potato" look to him.

The detective parked alongside the curb, and the young man approached the passenger door of the car. He leaned down and asked through the open window, "Are you Detective Snow? I'm David Stone; you wanted to talk to me?"

"Hello David," the detective responded. "Get in, we can talk right here in the car." They sat in the unmarked police car and had a conversation that Detective Snow tape-recorded. David Stone struck the detective as a young man trying to elevate his own self-importance. He was openly boastful of his knowledge of gold and silver and his financial dealings. He was also outwardly nervous, as evidenced by his rapid-fire answers and what appeared to be an attempt to divert suspicion away from himself. During this conversation, Stone related that James Bibee was a good friend and that they regularly met at Stone's house to trade coins because Mr. Bibee did not like to trade coins in the shop, where someone might view them. He went on to state that on Thursday evening, "Mr. Bibee arrived at my house at about five in the evening and I traded some of my Byzantine coins for some silver dollars."

David was quick to indicate that his wife, Betsy, was present when Mr. Bibee came to the house, although she remained in the kitchen and was not in the room where the transactions occurred. Following this exchange, Stone said that he then assisted Bibee in carrying boxes containing his collection, placing them on the front seat of the old Chevrolet, whereupon Mr. Bibee drove away.

Stone then said, "But you know, he did stop and pick up some guy at the corner. This guy flagged him down and they talked a second, then he got into the car and they drove away." When asked to describe this person, he said he was too far away to see him well but said he was of average height and weight, had dark hair and appeared "young looking." Again, he quickly added that his wife was inside the residence and did not see Mr. Bibee leave and did not see him pick up anybody at the corner. He said that upon returning to the house, he remembered mentioning this to his wife because he, David, never picked up hitchhikers.

Gary Snow pointed out that if Mr. Bibee was careful enough not to trade coins in his office, it would seem unusual for him to pick up a hitchhiker, especially with the coin collection sitting on the front seat of his car. Stone said he just assumed Mr. Bibee knew the person since the subject waved and talked to him on the driver's side of the vehicle before getting into the passenger's side. Stone then agreed with Snow's statement that it was somewhat coincidental that Bibee would run into someone he knew just a few houses away from Stone's residence. An experienced investigator, Detective Snow immediately became suspicious of David Stone.

David said that he first learned of Mr. Bibee's disappearance when Tom Duffy called Thursday evening, August 2, inquiring about Mr. Bibee's whereabouts. He said Tom Duffy told him over the phone that Mr. Bibee wasn't seen after he left the Stone residence that evening. David then commented, "How does he know anybody didn't see him after he left my place?"

Detective Snow asked David Stone if he would mind coming to the detective division in order to talk to his partner, Detective Hickman, about the case. He agreed. While en route, the detective stopped at the rear parking lot of the Denny's Restaurant, next to the canal where some of the coins had been tossed, to contact and pick up Detective Hickman. Detective Snow wrote in his report, "David Stone acted rather nervous after observing the officers standing by the location of the recovered coins."

At headquarters, David Stone repeated the same basic story he had given to Detective Snow and continually embellished it by stating that he was a good friend of Mr. Bibee and that "we often did transactions at my home." He continued to insist that his wife, Betsy, was in the house when Mr. Bibee was there. During the interview, Stone was asked if he would submit to a polygraph examination to show that he was being completely truthful concerning the information he had given. David said that he was "very reluctant" to take one. He became nervous and stated that he didn't believe in polygraph examinations, as he believed they were not accurate. At this time, the detectives advised David of his Miranda rights. He stated that he understood them and was willing to answer any questions.

He was then asked where he had been Saturday, August 4. David was reluctant to say where he had been that day, saying it was a personal matter and that he didn't see how that related to the missing person. A short time later, he stated that he had spent most of the day "just walking around in the Manchester and Fashion Fair Mall areas doing some thinking." This was in contrast to a statement he had given earlier that he and his wife had been together most of the day. Detective Snow wrote in his report, "It should be noted that David Stone had become very evasive in answering questions."

After about an hour into the interview, David Stone said he wanted to call his father about the possibility of taking a polygraph. He was allowed to do so, and after having a discussion with his father, David told the detectives that he did not want to take a polygraph, did not want to make any further statements and wanted to consult an attorney.

Sunday and Monday went by with no further leads on the whereabouts of James Bibee or his old Chevrolet. Detective Snow spoke with Betsy Stone, David's wife. She reiterated what her husband had said about the meeting at their house and that Mr. Bibee left their house sometime around 6:00 p.m. that evening. She said that she did not pay much attention to their dealings and could add nothing more. Although Detective Snow did not know it at the time, Betsy Stone's statement that she was present in the house during this meeting between her husband and Mr. Bibee would become significant a few years later.

Detective Snow also talked to Harold Kelley, the friend of both Tom Duffy and James Bibee. He told the detective that he had gone to Duffy's antique store in the morning hours of August 2, somewhere between 11:30 a.m. and noon. He said that David Stone was there when he arrived and that Stone and Bibee were just ending a conversation that appeared to be about trading some coins. Stone left the business at that time. About an hour later, Mr. Bibee received a telephone call. Kelley said that he assumed it was from David Stone since he heard James Bibee tell the person on the phone that he would come by after work.

In an attempt to gather further information regarding Bibee's visit to the Stone residence, Detective Snow, along with another Fresno Police Department detective, John Reynolds, decided that they needed to contact David Stone's neighbors. One of those neighbors they contacted was a woman by the name of Maxine Guthrie. She and her family lived two houses from the Stone residence on Backer Street. The neighborhood was one of middle-class tract homes located a few blocks from Fresno State University.

Mrs. Guthrie told the detectives that she was playing with her children in the front yard of her home that Thursday evening while awaiting her husband to arrive from work. She said she recalled David Stone walking past her home. It appeared to her that David had something of a worried or distressed look on his face, and she thought that something was wrong with him. In his hands, he was carrying a red-colored cloth or handkerchief. She further indicated that she said hello to him as he walked by but received no answer. Mrs. Guthrie informed them that she recalled Stone left his residence by car that evening while it was still daylight but she could not recall whether this was before or after she saw him walking.

Gary Snow and fellow detectives of the Fresno Police Department worked every lead they could find trying to locate the missing coin dealer. Missing person bulletins were put out to all police agencies in the state describing James Bibee and his old Chevrolet. The police department received many calls from people who had read about the disappearance in the newspaper or heard about it on the radio and thought they had seen either Mr. Bibee or his car.

Tuesday, August 7, was one of those typical Central Valley summer days when the temperature hits the high nineties by noon and then gets hotter. Detective Snow was en route to the police station after having checked out a call from someone who thought they had a lead on the Bibee disappearance when he was contacted by the police dispatcher. He was advised that Bibee's old Chevrolet had been located in the 400 block of Baron Street in the adjoining city of Clovis—in fact, it was parked directly across the street from the Clovis Police Department. Dispatch also informed him that the vehicle had a foul-smelling odor about it and possible body fluids leaking from the trunk.

Upon arrival at the scene, he found that the vehicle was being watched over by two Clovis police officers. Apparently, the first time anyone had become aware of it was about 4:10 p.m. that afternoon, some ten to twenty minutes before Snow arrived. The husband of one of the secretaries employed at the police department had arrived at that hour to pick up his wife. He was accompanied by another man, and when they parked in front of the building, they were overcome by the foul odor emanating from the faded brown, 1964 Chevrolet Impala parked in front of them. They reported this to the dispatcher, who in turn ran a record check on the license number. It came back registered to James Bibee of Fresno, California.

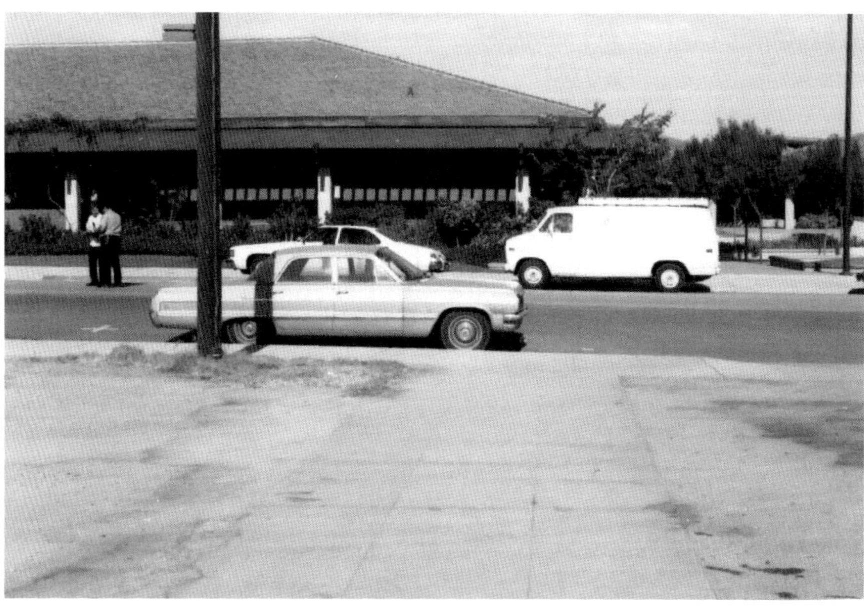

James Bibee's brown Chevrolet parked in front of the Clovis Police Department. *Courtesy of Fresno Police Department.*

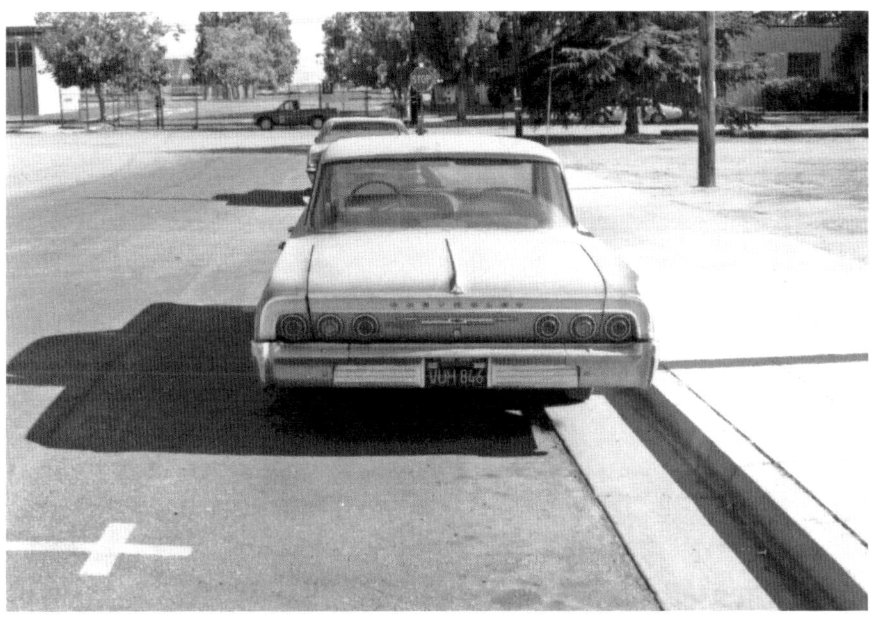

Rear view of the brown Chevrolet parked in front of the Clovis Police Department. *Courtesy of Fresno Police Department.*

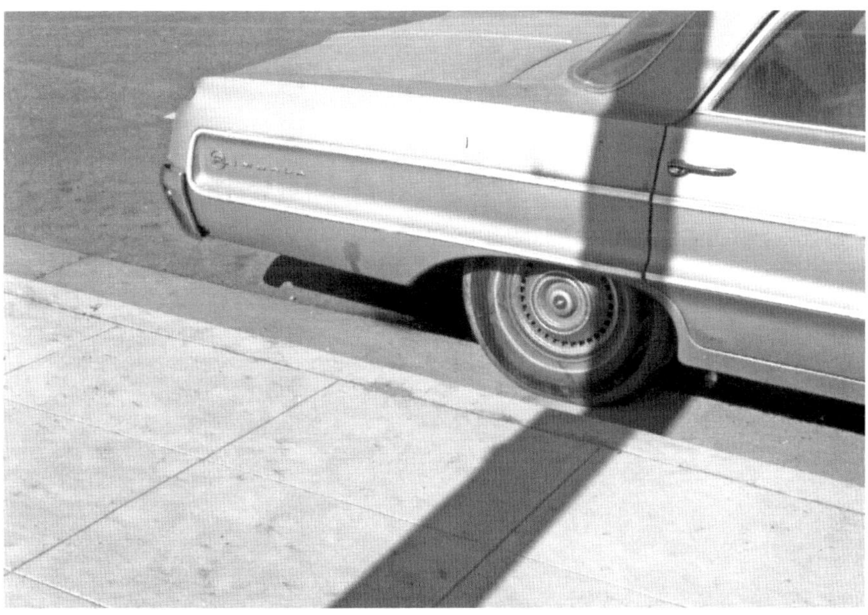

Side view of the brown Chevrolet, with bodily fluids leaking out of trunk area. *Courtesy of Fresno Police Department.*

The vehicle was legally parked along the west curb on Baron Street facing a southerly direction. No one had reportedly touched it. Snow's subsequent report reflected that the driver's door was unlocked and the window rolled down and the front passenger door as well as both back doors were locked and the windows rolled up. Oddly enough, the transmission was in the drive rather than the park position. There were no keys in the ignition. Further, there were no citations on the vehicle and no indication that the tires had been marked by the police for a possible parking violation. A light film of dust or dirt covered the vehicle except at the trunk area, where there were possible fabric or scuff marks, indicating that someone either had wiped this area or had brushed up against it.

After twelve years of police work, Snow knew that the odor from the trunk area was the smell of death. He requested the Fresno police dispatcher to have a patrol unit contact Nell Bibee and obtain a set of keys for the trunk. While awaiting the arrival of the keys, Snow inventoried the contents of the vehicle's interior. He found several items of debris scattered about: a box of Kleenex tissues, several pieces of tissue, old newspapers, a can of window cleaner, a can of carburetor cleaner, an old glove, a white rag and a red thermos.

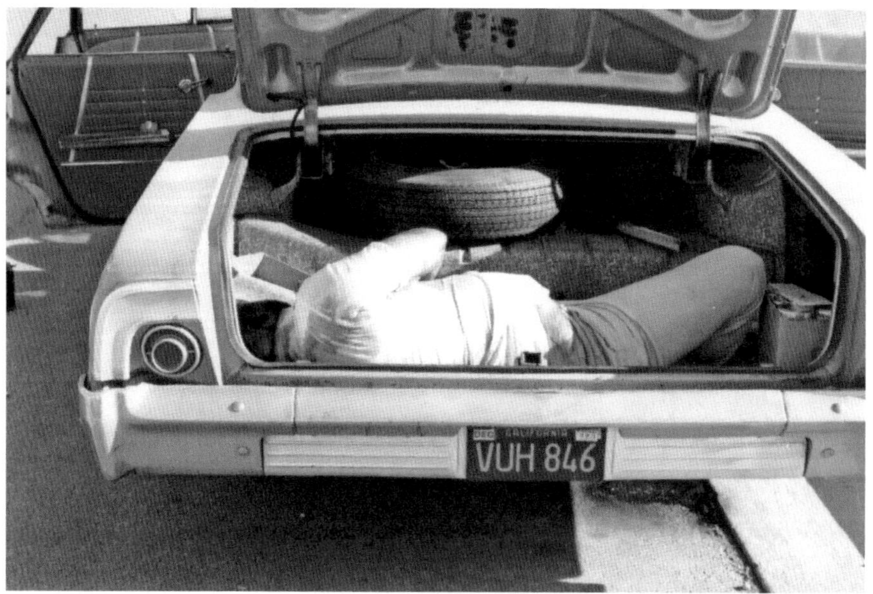

James Bibee's body found in the trunk of the brown Chevrolet. *Courtesy of Fresno Police Department.*

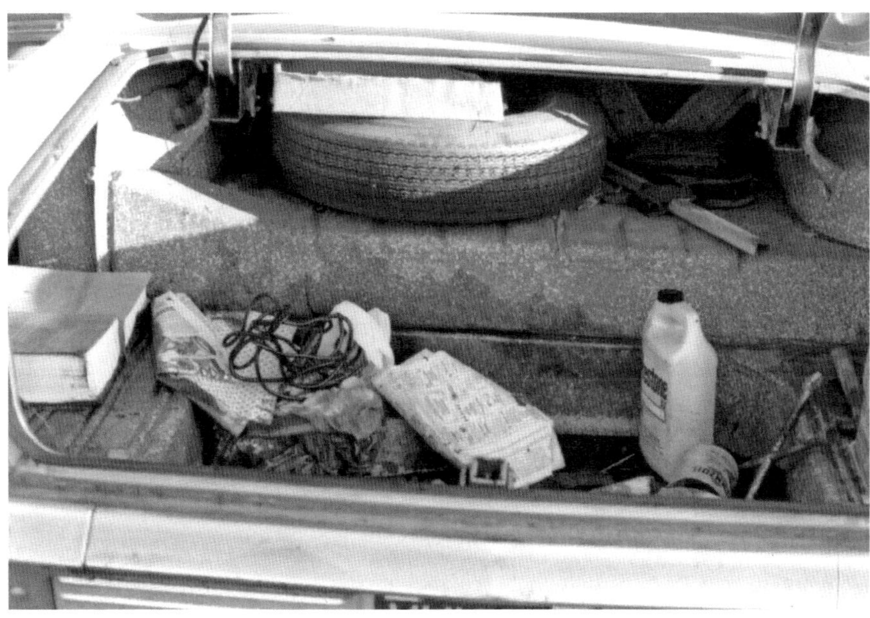

Trunk of the brown Chevrolet after victim's body was removed. *Courtesy of Fresno Police Department.*

When the extra set of keys arrived, Gary Snow's suspicions were confirmed. Inside the trunk was the fully clothed body of James Bibee. He was lying on his side in a fetal position, and his body appeared to be in the early stages of decomposition, as evidenced by the bloated condition and discoloration. The gruesome sight was compounded by the numerous maggots around the head and neck area.

On the ring finger of his left hand, he wore a gold wedding band, and a gold-colored wristwatch was on his left wrist. In the trouser pockets, the officers removed some miscellaneous change, a packet of heart pills and a pocket knife. However, there was no wallet found.

The Bibee Autopsy

An autopsy was conducted on Wednesday, August 8, the day after discovery of the body. It was performed by Dr. Thomas Nelson, a pathologist who had been conducting autopsies for Fresno County and surrounding counties for nearly thirty-five years and was conceded to be an authority on matters relating to causes of death. In fact, he was often called as an expert witness by both the prosecution and the defense in cases wherein there was a controversy regarding a cause of death, the time of death or the condition of a body based on its location following death.

The autopsy determined that James Bibee was a white adult male who appeared to be his stated age of seventy-two years. He measured six feet tall and weighed approximately 170 pounds. For all that Dr. Nelson could conclude by his examination, Mr. Bibee appeared to be in good health other than the stated heart problems that were being treated with medication.

The autopsy revealed that James Bibee died as the result of ten .22-caliber bullet wounds, all to the upper chest area. Dr. Nelson formed the opinion that the first two rounds were fired at the victim as both he and his assailant were standing somewhat side by side. This determination was made primarily by the angles of entry and the tracks taken by the bullets after entry. He then concluded that the remaining eight rounds were fired into the victim after he was down on his back and his assailant stood over him. The angles of entry were used by the pathologist to form this opinion, along with the proximity of these rounds to one another. Also considered was the fact that the chest area was hemorrhaging and full of blood before these last eight shots entered.

Of special interest to Detective Snow was the pathologist's opinion relating to the stage of decomposition. Due to the fact that the victim's fingertips were dry and dark and exhibited some stage of mummification, Dr. Nelson indicated that the body had not been in the hot automobile trunk for an extended length of time. Further evidence of this fact was that some of the muscles of the lower extremities were not as decomposed as the head area. "These conditions cause me to form the opinion that the deceased had been in a cooler location than the location in which he was found for some period of time following death," wrote Dr. Nelson in his autopsy report. He further concluded that based on the degree of decomposition, the victim had been dead between three and seven days when discovered.

What had started out as a missing person report some five days before had now become a murder investigation.

Focusing on a Suspect

Detectives Snow and Reynolds were experienced homicide investigators. They both agreed that their most obvious suspect in the murder of James Bibee was David Stone, as he was apparently the last person known to have seen Mr. Bibee alive. He had, in fact, invited the victim to his home that evening, something that the victim's friends said they had never known him to do. Added to this was that his behavior on the evening of Mr. Bibee's disappearance was described by Maxine Guthrie as being strange and suspicious. They also both agreed that they lacked that one piece of physical evidence or that one witness necessary to make an arrest.

Neither of them believed David's story about some hitchhiker or anything else he had told them, yet they could not find that one telltale flaw in his story. It was their opinion that the key to the case for the time being was the suspect's wife, Betsy Stone. As Snow expressed it, "She's either involved somehow or totally naive." Determined to find some inconsistency in the stories about Bibee's fateful visit, they returned that evening to the house of David and Betsy Stone.

The evening was warm when the detectives arrived at the Stone's Backer Street address. David Stone was in the front yard as they drove up and parked alongside the curb. Detective Snow advised him that they were not there to talk to him since he had previously indicated he wanted to consult with an attorney, adding that they were there to speak to his wife. Just as David was telling them that his wife was not home, Betsy Stone drove around the corner and into the driveway. She appeared nervous as she agreed to speak with the detectives and invited them into the house.

Betsy told them she had known James Bibee ever since she had gotten married some two and a half years earlier. She said he had often come to their residence to trade coins with her husband. In fact, he had been there as recently as one month prior to the visit on August 2. She further indicated that she stayed in the other room while the victim and her husband were trading coins that Thursday and that she did not hear him leave. Her husband had walked Mr. Bibee to his car when he left and, upon returning to the house, mentioned that Mr. Bibee had picked up someone at the corner. She said the reason her husband mentioned this was because he himself never picked up hitchhikers. In answer to questioning, she said her husband did take a walk later that evening, as he had been advised by his doctor to walk because of high blood pressure.

Detective Snow indicated in his report of the interview with Betsy Stone that David Stone was present and "had attempted to interject into the conversation a couple of times." When the two detectives left the Stone residence that evening, they were convinced that David Stone was their man and that his wife was covering up for him, yet as Snow said, "We just need that one piece of evidence."

Part III
THE MOYER INVESTIGATION

The New Investigator

Barbara Wittman hated it when her husband was involved in a police undercover narcotic operation. During these times, he would let his hair grow, go unshaven, wear "scroungy" clothes and sunglasses and generally look like a lowlife. He had been conducting such an operation for several months when he was assigned to the Moyer homicide. The operation, which involved three other undercover narcotic officers and an informant, was designed to make drug purchases from dealers on the north side of Visalia.

It was this "scraggly looking biker-type," as Barbara described him, who went to dinner with her in some of San Francisco's finest restaurants during their vacation. However, as she later explained it to some of her friends, "I was really embarrassed, but you know what a 'ham' Bill is, he really played the part. The waiters all thought he was some kind of Hells Angel and one place even refused to serve us until Bill started making such a scene and threatened to sue."

Bill Wittman was a "ham," but it was his ability to play a role that made him such an effective investigator. He could play the hard, intimidating cop role when necessary just as easily as he could be the cajoling, buddy-buddy type to whom criminal suspects would readily confess their innermost secrets. Perhaps his most effective role was when he played the poor, dumb country bumpkin who always appears to be outsmarted. He was something of a Columbo from the popular television series of a few years ago. When playing this role, he would put on his best Oklahoma, "good ol' boy" accent.

He was an excellent con man, actor or role player, whichever label one would choose. A fellow investigator often told a story about a trip he and Wittman took to Oklahoma City to find and bring back to Visalia a petty thief and drunk named Jeremy Martinez. Martinez was a percipient witness to a murder and was needed to testify. Frightened of the prospect of testifying, he had fled to his hometown of Oklahoma City.

After determining that their man had been seen in the skid row district, Wittman and his partner went to that area of town. It was January and extremely cold when they happened upon an abandoned warehouse in which some fifteen to twenty transients were huddled together trying to keep warm around a small fire inside an old oil barrel. Desiring to question these men about Martinez, Wittman unhesitatingly walked right up to the group. Some of the men stood up and backed away, ready to flee. Others glared menacingly at him, while a few reached inside their coats, apparently for weapons.

Rather than identify himself as a police officer, Wittman, in a loud voice announced, "Fellas, my name is Hud Wilson and I own this here building. Y'all are welcome to sleep here outa the cold so long as ya don' wreck nothin'."

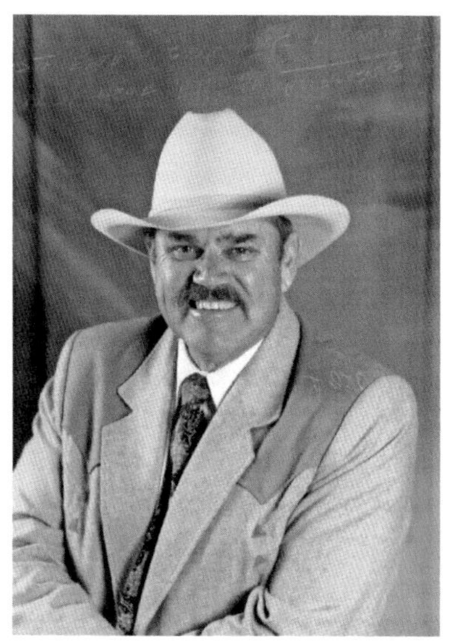

Bill Wittman. *Courtesy of Sue Gunderman, sheriff's executive assistant, Tulare County Sheriff's Department.*

One of those who was about to flee walked forward and, relieved that he was not about to be rousted or arrested, said, "Thanks Mr. Wilson, we sure do 'preciate that."

"Yah," said another. "Don' worry, we'll take good care of yer buildin'."

Instantly, all the men felt welcome and relaxed. As Wittman and his partner were leaving the building, he turned and said to the group, "Oh, by the way, I'm lookin' for an ol' boy by name of Jeremy Martinez. Have y'all seen him?"

"Whatta ya want him for, is he in trouble?" asked one of the group.

"Oh no," replied Wittman. "I gotta job for him in my truckin' business."

Trustingly, the man said, "I just saw him at Mamie's Café over on fifty-second street." Within an hour, they had their man and were en route back to Visalia.

Regardless of what role he was playing, one thing was constant: nearly everyone liked Bill Wittman. A natural extrovert, he would talk to anyone about anything. His wife often commented that just sending him to the store could take hours because he was sure to run into someone he knew and start talking. In fact, he did not even have to know them. The truth of the matter was that Bill Wittman most likely could not go anywhere in Visalia without running into someone he knew. A cop with fourteen years on the police force in a small town would naturally become acquainted with many people. Add to this Bill Wittman's outgoing personality and his being the lead singer in a country western band and it was not surprising that he was so well known.

The band, called A Six Pack and a Half Pint, was originally started by a group of local police officers. For some reason nobody could quite remember, Wittman was either asked or volunteered to be the lead singer. Despite never having sung in any organized group, he performed well. With a good voice, an instinctive sense of rhythm and timing and a natural flair for showmanship, he soon became the star of the show. He performed equally well doing a sad Hank Williams song such as "Mansion on the Hill" or rocking into Elvis Presley's "Heartbreak Hotel." The band would play at various dances for a fee and would often perform free at charity events. The group got so good that by the summer of 1979 it was performing an average of three times per month. Its notoriety was enhanced by a three-page write-up, complete with photographs, in the *Visalia Times-Delta*. After the band broke up in the early 1990s, Bill often sang at Ritchie's Barn with a country-western band led by a local rancher, Clarence Ritchie.

Born in Oklahoma, Wittman came to California's Central Valley with his mother and grandparents as an infant. Looking for work, they followed the harvest trail, picking fruit and vegetables as transient laborers. His grandfather finally obtained a steady job as a farmhand, and the family settled in the city of Tulare. Young Bill, an only child, nevertheless grew up in a large family with grandparents, aunts, uncles and cousins; his alcoholic father remained in Oklahoma.

Growing up in Tulare, he worked in the fields picking cotton. Upon graduation from high school, the first in his family ever to do so, he went to work as an apprentice butcher. Bored with the "lack of adventure" in the life of a butcher, he applied for and was accepted as a police officer for the City of Visalia.

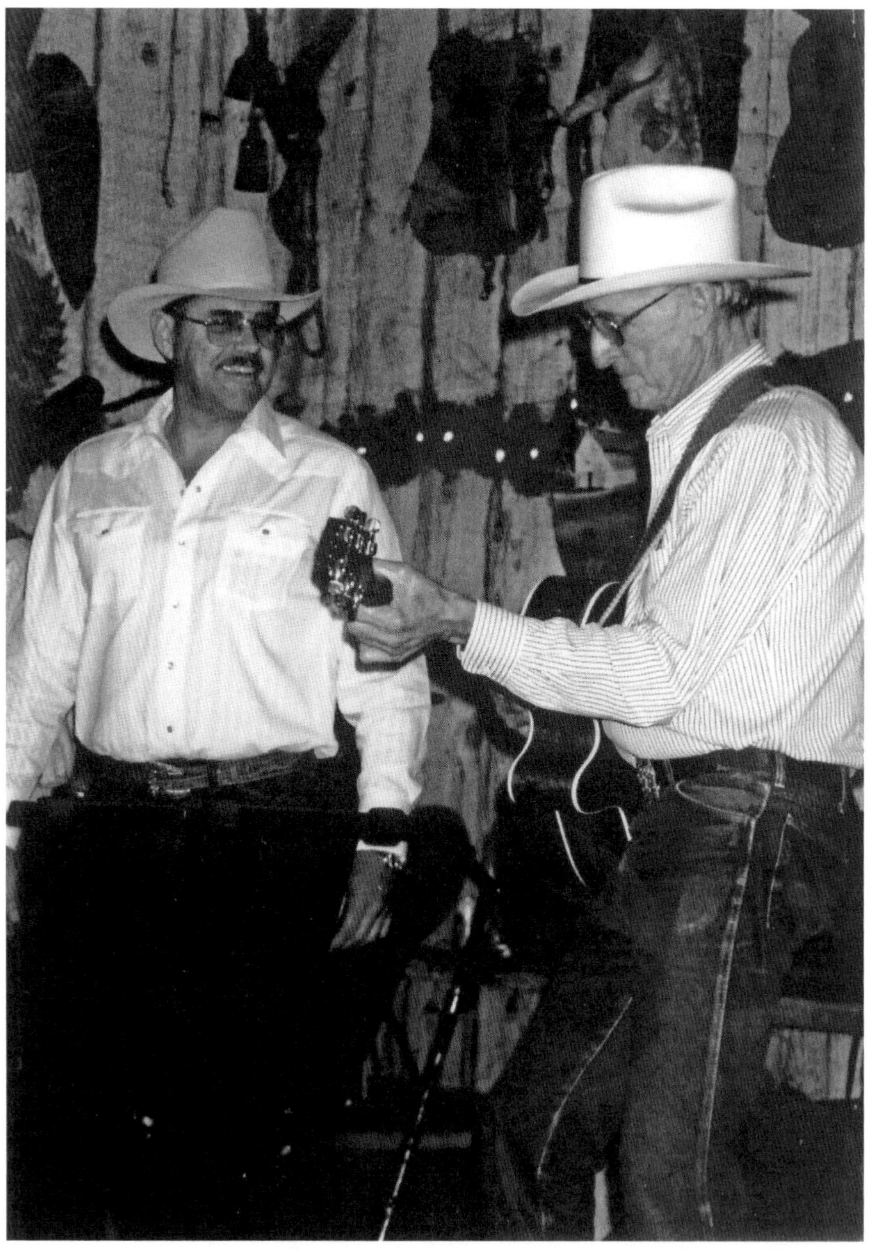

Bill Wittman with Clarence Ritchie at Ritchie's Barn. *Courtesy of Sue Gunderman, sheriff's executive assistant, Tulare County Sheriff's Department.*

A scrawny little kid as a youngster and teenager, he started lifting weights in his early twenties and filled out his five-foot, eight-inch frame to 180 pounds. He had a large barrel chest that looked all the larger when viewed with his skinny legs. The years of weightlifting had made his hands and arms strong, and he was respected among his fellow officers, as well as by the "dudes on the street," as one who was more than able to take care of himself in a scuffle.

As a rookie cop, Bill ended up in many scuffles with arrestees, tough guys, cop haters and more; however, as he would say, "I got tired of all that fightin' business. It's a whole lot easier talkin' than fightin." Even though he no longer got into any scuffles, an old-timer on the police department named Lloyd Monroe, in his slow Arkansas drawl, would describe Bill as "a lil' ol' banty rooster." This description was in reference to Wittman's manner of walk—a sort of strut, giving the appearance of cockiness, the little man who won't take anything from anyone, particularly some street punk. As Lloyd said, "His walk was like that of a banty rooster."

Many of the long hours put in by police detectives pass in boredom. Long drives to follow up leads, stakeouts and the like consume many unproductive hours. However, there was little boredom when spending time with Bill Wittman. Ever the talker, he would keep up a steady stream of conversation, ranging from the case at hand to storytelling, much of which concerned his family.

Another source of Wittman stories was his experiences involved in police work. When related by Wittman, any story took on a humorous quality. He had an arsenal of Lloyd Monroe stories and kept his fellow officers in stitches relating them. Monroe was a "good ol' Arky boy" who had been in police work some fifteen years. Tall, his head full of once-black hair now turned silver, with a thin moustache, he looked strikingly like the entertainer and actor Tennessee Ernie Ford. Friendly and soft-spoken, Lloyd had a knack for ending up in unusual and often hilarious situations, and Bill related them with regularity.

One of his favorite stories took place when Wittman was assigned the investigation of a prostitution operation that advertised in the local Visalia newspaper as an escort service. Upon calling the number, the arrangements for an "escort" could be made, and the "escort" would then agree to meet her customer at his apartment or motel room. Although not a sophisticated or professional operation, it nevertheless was the source of complaints by several of the citizenry in the conservative community—hence Wittman's assignment.

The plan was to make the necessary arrangements over the phone, have her come to a local motel room in which an undercover officer would be lying in bed. He would then further engage the woman in conversation wherein a more definitive solicitation for an act of prostitution would hopefully be made by her. Wittman and another officer would be hidden in the closet. Upon hearing the solicitation, they would exit, identify themselves as police officers and make an arrest.

The person chosen to lie in bed and engage the potential arrestee in conversation was Lloyd Monroe. At this time, Lloyd had been temporarily working the parking control beat in uptown Visalia, which involved patrolling the uptown area in a small golf cart and ticketing vehicles that remained parked beyond the posted time limit. All the arrangements had been made. Wittman had called the escort service, identified himself as Hud Wilson (his favorite alias) and agreed to wait for his escort in a certain motel room that he had previously rented. He was hidden in the closet along with another officer named Gabe Rodriguez, and Lloyd was lying in bed when there came a knock on the door.

Lloyd said, "Come in."

Wittman heard the door open and a woman's voice exclaim, "Lloyd what are you doing here?"

Lloyd could then be heard saying, "Gawd damn Wilma I didn' expect you."

As Wittman then explained, "Me an' ol Gabe started laughin' and the whole thing fell apart." It turned out that the woman worked at a small newspaper and magazine shop in uptown Visalia, and Lloyd had been trying to get a date with her just the day before. Using his best imitation of Lloyd's Arkansas drawl, Wittman said that Lloyd told him, "Honest Willie, ah didn' know she was that type-a woman. Gawd damn, she's gonna starve if she has to sell that thing."

One of the qualities that made Bill Wittman an effective investigator, along with his ability to relate to people, was the effort he put into his investigations. Investigators or detectives, whatever designation one wants to use, are no different than people in other lines of employment. Some are tireless and hard-driving, willing to make that extra effort in performing their jobs, while others are just plain lazy, content to sit back and hope that the case somehow solves itself. Wittman was definitely the former. In his own low-key way he would follow up each and every lead, no matter how remote it might seem. To the casual observer, this bull-doggedness would not be apparent.

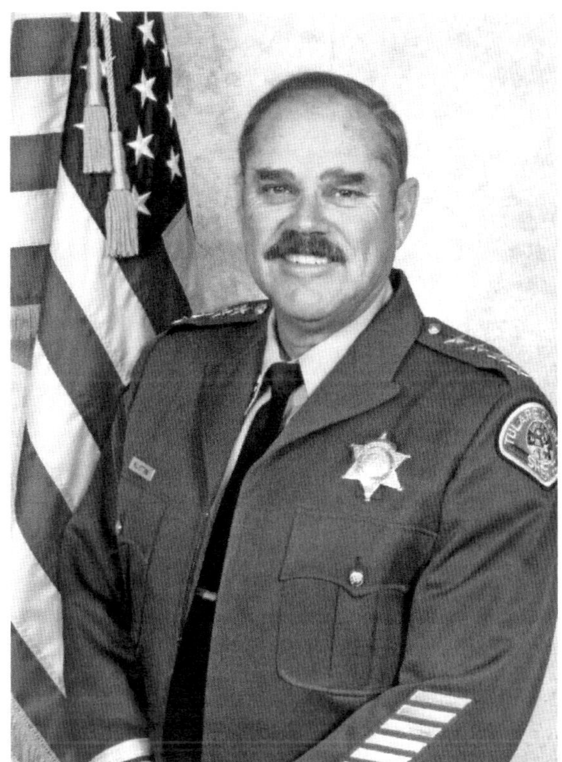

Right: Bill Wittman was elected Tulare County sheriff in 1995. *Courtesy of Sue Gunderman, sheriff's executive assistant, Tulare County Sheriff's Department.*

Below: Sheriff Bill Wittman with some members of group known as the "Tulare County Sheriff's Posse." *Courtesy of Sue Gunderman, sheriff's executive assistant, Tulare County Sheriff's Department.*

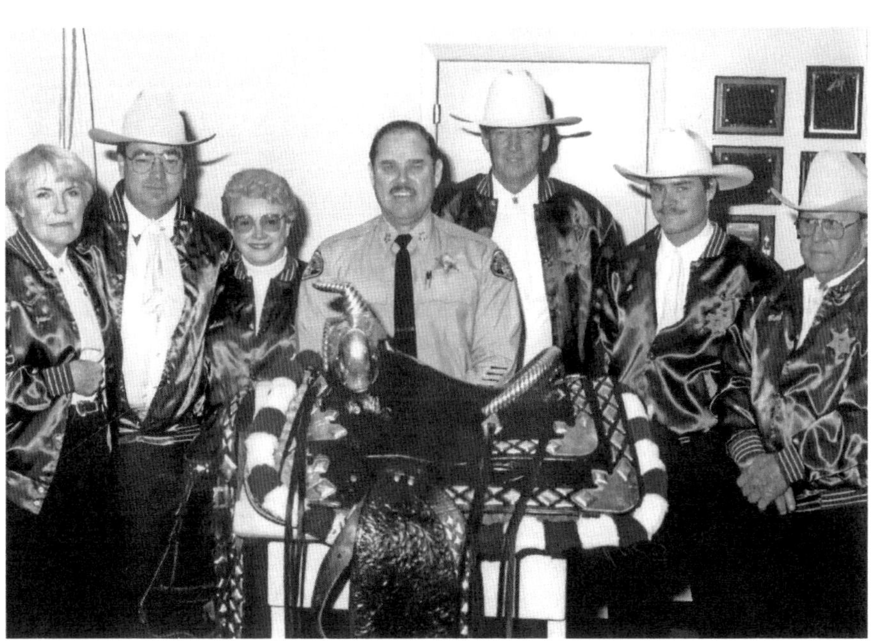

Unlike John Calvin, Wittman did not scurry around in a nervous frenzy, chain-smoking and drinking countless cups of coffee. He would more likely be found leaning back in his chair with his feet, adorned in one of his many pair of cowboy boots, resting on top of his desk. As Bill McGowen would discover, it was this propensity for toughness and tenacity, disguised though it may be, that would produce the killer of James Bibee and Alex Moyer.

At age thirty-eight, Bill Wittman still enjoyed police work. He liked people and enjoyed meeting and helping them. In addition, he liked the intrigue of certain police activities, such as undercover operations or investigating interesting cases. He thought the Moyer homicide was just such a case and looked forward to the challenge it presented. Little did he realize at the time just how unusual a suspect he was soon to encounter.

DETECTIVES MEET THEIR SUSPECT

When a police agency has a certain type of crime with no apparent suspect, it will often put out a teletype to other agencies describing the facts of the crime. Because some criminal offenders will commit several crimes with the same or similar method of operation (modus operandi), this serves as a means of communicating with other agencies that may have had the same or a similar crime committed in their jurisdiction. By pooling their information and working in conjunction with one another, police agencies have a greater chance of determining the identity of the responsible person or persons.

Soon after the Moyer homicide, such a teletype was sent out by the Visalia Police Department describing the victim as a coin dealer, the fact that he was shot by a .22-caliber firearm in his coin shop during an apparent robbery and the lack of any struggle or forced entry. It could be that this was just a robbery-murder without regard to any pattern or particular type of victim; however, it might be part of a given "m.o." that had occurred in another area.

In mid-November 1979, Fresno police detective Gary Snow was sifting through a batch of teletypes that had been received when the Moyer teletype caught his eye. Although the facts were not necessarily the same, nevertheless, it was similar to the Bibee murder. It just might be that the same person was responsible for both crimes and a combination of the available clues could lead to a suspect. With this in mind, he called the Visalia Police Department.

After identifying himself and asking to speak to the investigator handling the Moyer homicide, he was transferred to Sergeant Wittman's phone. "We've got a coin dealer murder here that happened a couple of months before yours," he explained to Wittman. "It could be it's the same guy. Do you have any suspects?"

"Hell no," answered Wittman. "We don't have a thing 'cept a dead body. What've you got?"

Snow explained that they had one suspect who was the last person to see the victim alive but that they did not have enough evidence to arrest him. "He's a strong suspect but we're just missing that one piece to really go after him," Snow said. They agreed to meet, go over their respective reports and discuss the two cases, for as Wittman said, "Any lead is better than what we have now."

A few days later, Wittman and McGowen drove the forty-five miles to Fresno and met with Gary Snow in his office at the Fresno Police Department. The three compared the similarities between the two crimes. Both victims were coin dealers, robbery appeared to be the apparent motive in both cases and both were killed by someone who had gained their confidence, as there appeared to be no signs of a fight or struggle surrounding either incident. Additionally, as Gary Snow remarked, "What bothers me is that here's two coin dealers killed within two months, in cities less than an hour apart, and I haven't heard of a coin dealer being killed in all the years I've been on the P.D. It could be just a coincidence, but it sure seems strange."

"Who's this guy Stone?" asked Wittman.

"He's sort of a peach-fuzz little guy," answered Snow, "a big talker. His story about our victim picking up some guy at the corner near his house is b.s. I pass by that area on my way to work and there's no pedestrian traffic in that area. Stone's street T's into Sierra Avenue and it's all residences on his street and the north side of Sierra. Across on the south side of Sierra is a large cotton field. There's just no way anyone would be walking in that area. Besides our victim wasn't the type to pick up anyone."

McGowen then asked Snow if he suspected Stone's wife to be involved. "Because from the way I understand your case, if Stone was responsible, she had to know."

"You're right," responded Snow. "She's gotta know or be part of it. She was real nervous in discussing the dealings at her house that evening. I really think she might crack if we could get to her. But hell, we don't even have enough to arrest him, let alone her."

Wittman asked if David Stone had any police contacts in the past. "We can't find anything, not even a traffic ticket," replied Snow.

On the ride back to Visalia, the two detectives discussed their case and compared it further to the Fresno murder. "Well, at least we got one lead," Wittman said. "Fresno's suspect is a coin dealer too, maybe he's done business with Moyer. Tomorrow let's go through all of Moyer's records and look for his name. And how 'bout lets go to the D.A. and get a search warrant for his phone records. If he called Moyer from Fresno it oughta show up as a toll call."

The next day, Wittman drafted an affidavit for a search warrant. This affidavit set forth the probable cause necessary to support the issuance of the search warrant. The purpose of the warrant was to obtain from the Pacific Telephone Company the billing records for David Stone's telephone and the U.S. Stamp and Coin telephone from July 1, 1979, through October 31, 1979. The warrant was signed by a Tulare County judge and served on Pacific Telephone.

These billing records provided a history of long-distance telephone calls from a given telephone number by showing the date and time of day the call was made, the duration of the call in minutes and the city, state and telephone number called. The billing also reflected whether the call was placed from a number other than the telephone number billed. Should a call be placed from a public telephone and charged to the number for which the billing was provided, this was shown. However, when this occurred, the time the call was placed was not shown, although the date of the call was indicated.

It was late February 1980 when the records from Pacific Telephone were received by Sergeant Wittman. Upon reviewing David Stone's telephone billings, he noted calls on September 4, 6 and 27, 1979, to the U.S. Stamp and Coin Shop. Even more significantly, the billings showed two calls from Stone's number to Alex Moyer's shop the week preceding the murder. The first was placed on Tuesday, October 2, 1979, at 4:45 p.m. and lasted for nine minutes. The second was made on Thursday, October 4, 1979, at 2:37 p.m. and lasted for twelve minutes.

"Look at these calls," Wittman beckoned to McGowen. "Didn't that one fella say that Moyer had some deal set up with a guy from Fresno?"

"Yeah, that older guy, Henry somethin' or other, said Moyer told him that somebody from Fresno was gonna buy all his gold coins. The deal was set for Friday and changed to Saturday. Ya know, we haven't connected Moyer to anyone from Fresno yet."

"Well this looks like a start," exclaimed Wittman. "I think we oughta take a ride to Fresno and visit this David Stone character."

It was 11:00 a.m. on Tuesday, March 4, 1980, when Detectives Wittman and McGowen rang the doorbell at the residence that David and Betsy Stone rented on North Backer Street in Fresno. About one minute later, the door was opened by the person who would soon become the prime suspect in the Moyer murder.

"Are you David Stone?" asked Wittman.

"Yes, what can I do for you?" answered the young man. "You're not here on the Bibee case are you?" he quickly added. "I've been advised by my attorney not to talk about the Bibee case or the Visalia case."

Both Wittman and McGowen were somewhat taken aback by the reference to the Visalia case, since as far as they knew, no one had contacted him about it. "What's your attorney's name?" McGowen inquired.

David Stone responded that the last name was Farnsworth; however, he could not recall his first name nor his address. Then he stated, "This is actually my father's attorney but he's advising me." A few seconds passed as the two detectives sized up this individual who appeared to be so closely linked to the Bibee murder. After all their years in police work and dealing with hard-core criminals, this was not what they expected their potential suspect to look like. Blond-haired, blue eyed and of fair complexion, he looked more like a sophomore in high school who had not yet begun to shave rather than a twenty-three-year-old man suspected of murder. Standing five feet, seven inches, small in stature and somewhat overweight, he did not appear to be a physical or outdoorsy kind of person. Bill Wittman soon began referring to him as the "Pillsbury Doughboy."

After a short pause, David Stone broke the silence by stating, "Okay, I guess I'll talk to you about the Visalia case. Come on in." They entered the living room, where Wittman and McGowen took a seat on the couch and Stone, after hesitating a moment, sat down in a chair facing the two detectives. He again announced that he would discuss only the Visalia case and did not want to talk about the Bibee case because, as he put it, the Fresno officers had mistreated him by "roughing me up and trying to trick me into saying something that wasn't true."

When asked if he knew anything about the Moyer homicide, he stated that he did not—that, in fact, he and his wife had gone to Las Vegas that weekend, leaving Fresno on Saturday morning. As McGowen's report reflected, a small child was in the residence, and David Stone's wife, Betsy, was in and out of the living room. During most of the conversation, she stood just outside the door, obviously within hearing distance of the conversation. At one point, she entered the room and stated that she had a receipt for the

Travelodge Motel in South Las Vegas; however, the date was incorrect, as it listed them staying there on the seventh and eighth of October but should have read the sixth, seventh and eighth. David then interrupted and said that they did not stay at the Travelodge on the sixth; they stayed at the Fez Motel that night. He also added that he had received a traffic ticket between Bakersfield and Barstow for not having a sticker on his license plate.

The report by McGowen reflected that Stone insisted that they made no stops between Fresno and Las Vegas and arrived at 6:00 p.m. David Stone was a nonstop talker who would volunteer information even without being asked a question. He then made a statement that caught the interest of both Wittman and McGowen. He told the detectives that he recalled hearing a reference to the Moyer murder on the radio Sunday morning on October 7. This seemed strange since the body was discovered at about 8:30 a.m. on Sunday, and it would be much later in the day before the news of the murder would be released.

Both detectives noted that while discussing the Moyer murder, Stone became noticeably nervous. His hands would shake, his face became red and he would look away from them. They further noted an odd characteristic. During certain times in the conversation, he would blink repeatedly in almost a squinting manner. McGowan's report referred to this as a "twitch."

Stone stated that he dealt in gold coins but did not have any contact with U.S. Stamp and Coin; however, he had done business with Plunketts Coins in Visalia. A short while later, he stated that if he had any dealings with Alex Moyer, he could not remember it. After further conversation, Stone suddenly indicated that he did remember visiting Moyer's shop, believing that he may have purchased a small item and that his wife was with him. He then stated, somewhat inappropriately, "But that was before the murder."

Asked about his name appearing on a note found in Moyer's shop, David Stone became red in the face, began the rapid blinking and was noticeably nervous. He could not explain how this could be; however, he would check his records and get back to them if he could find anything. When asked about telephone calls to Moyer's shop the week before the murder, he could offer no explanation, only that he did a lot of calling to various coin dealers and may have called Moyer. Again he promised to "check my records and get back to you when I find something."

Just as they were preparing to leave, McGowen casually asked Stone why he thought Fresno police considered him a suspect in the Bibee case.

He said because Bibee was at his home the evening that he disappeared and that "I was the last one to see him alive, I mean the last one they know of." Asked why he thought the coins would be thrown away along the city streets, Stone responded rather curiously—he said this may have happened because the killer was probably a coin dealer and knew they were of little value. He then reiterated that he was mad at the Fresno police because they had "roughed him up."

Once they were inside their vehicle, Wittman announced, "Bill, I think this little doughboy is a killer."

"If he's not guilty he sure is trying his best to act like he is," responded McGowen. After the visit with David Stone and his wife, both Wittman and McGowen believed that Stone was very likely their killer. They went over the facts that pointed in his direction. David Stone had placed two telephone calls to Alex Moyer the week before the murder at very significant times.

The first was on Tuesday afternoon *after* Fred Sciacca's transaction with Moyer wherein Moyer offered to pay Sciacca in gold coins in an amount in excess of $2,000. Mr. Sciacca requested cash instead, so Moyer wrote him a check. The following day, on Wednesday afternoon, Moyer refused to sell Henry Lawson two gold coins. According to Lawson, the reason for this refusal was because a person from Fresno was coming on Friday to buy all his gold coins.

It was obvious that something had occurred between the Sciacca and Lawson visits to cause Alex Moyer to change his mind about selling gold coins. The detectives believed what occurred was a telephone call by David Stone to Moyer on Tuesday, after the transaction with Fred Sciacca, offering to buy all of his gold coins. In addition, there was a notation in Alex Moyer's writing of what purported to be a gold coin transaction involving a David from Fresno.

The second call from David Stone's telephone that week was on Thursday afternoon. This call coincided with Henry Lawson's explanation about returning to the coin shop on Friday afternoon and being told by Moyer that the appointment to buy all the gold coins had been changed from Friday to the next day, Saturday.

They had further learned that Stone and his wife left their infant daughter with his parents that Friday night, October 5. Although they were leaving for Las Vegas the next morning, rather than spend Friday night at their own residence, they stayed at a motel in Fresno. This seemed suspicious, as there was no reason to spend money on a motel room in their own hometown, especially in view of the fact that they were going to Las Vegas and presumably would want all their money available. The detectives could only conclude that this was an effort to conceal from the neighbors that Stone left in the early morning hours on Saturday to drive to Moyer's shop in Visalia and, as McGowan reasoned, to also provide an alibi since their motel bill showed they checked out at 10:58 a.m.

They also considered what they viewed as a strong case against David Stone in respect to the Bibee murder. Added to all these facts was the obvious nervousness exhibited by Stone when discussing either of these cases and some of his rather curious answers.

Bill Wittman believed that enough evidence was present to have a murder charge filed against David Stone, and in the hopes of getting a filing and an arrest warrant issued, he took the case to the Tulare County District Attorney's Office in the second week of March 1980. As he explained to the deputy district attorney reviewing the case, if he could just get a warrant to arrest Stone, he felt he would break and confess once he was placed into custody. However, the deputy rejected the case pending further investigation, as he explained, "You just need one more thing, a piece of physical evidence or some witness or something."

On Tuesday, April 1, Wittman was in his office going over some reports on another case when the phone rang. He answered, and Gary Snow was on the other end. "Guess what," he said. "Our little friend's been popped for a 211." The term "211" refers to the crime of robbery defined by California Penal Code Section 211. Snow went on to explain a most bizarre circumstance, the first of many that Wittman would become aware of involving David Stone.

Some sixteen months earlier, on December 28, 1978, a man walked into Randolph's Fine Jewelry Store in Clovis (a city adjacent to Fresno), said that he wanted to update his wife's wedding set and asked to see diamonds of approximately one karat. The man spent more than an hour looking at various diamonds and discussing with the sales clerk the characteristics of each. He then pulled a handgun from his jacket and calmly stated, "I can't make up my mind, I think I'll just take them all." The clerk obeyed his order to hand him the box of diamonds. The robber then fled on foot. The diamonds were valued at $25,000.

Snow then explained that on the previous Friday night, one of the jewelry store employees who was present at the robbery took his wife to the drive-in movie. As they pulled up to the ticket booth and he began to hand his money to the attendant, he noticed that the attendant was the same person who had robbed the jewelry store several months earlier. He contacted the police the next day and reported the incident and his identification.

Upon investigating, the police determined that David Stone was the movie attendant identified as the robber and that he had just begun employment. That Friday night was his first night of work. Stone apparently recognized the jewelry store employee and left work shortly after selling the ticket to him. David did not report to work on Saturday.

The police detectives contacted David Stone and obtained his fingerprints. They matched those left by the robber on the glass countertop of the jewelry store.

"And guess what," added Snow. "The name of the movie was *When Time Ran Out*. Pretty much describes it for the little SOB doesn't it?"

David Stone's father posted the bail, and he was released from custody on the jewelry robbery case. If the Fresno and Visalia detectives had any uncertainty of Stone's guilt in the Bibee and Moyer homicides, his being positively identified as responsible for the armed robbery convinced them that he was their man. Wittman was convinced that the "piece of evidence" necessary to build up the case so that the district attorney would file it would not be found in Visalia. There was no link to David Stone in Visalia other than what had been already recovered through telephone records and the note found in Moyer's shop. Even though Stone had indicated he had done business with Plunketts Coins in Visalia, there were no records of any transaction, and no one there could identify his picture or remember his name.

That One Piece of Evidence

Wittman and McGowen both reasoned that because Stone had no apparent source of income, he undoubtedly sold the coins they were convinced he stole from both Bibee and Moyer. To follow up, they set out to check all pawnshops and coin dealers in the Central Valley. Under California law, pawnbrokers are required to keep records of all transactions and submit them to the local police agency. They contacted the officer who covered the "fencing" detail for each police agency to determine if any pawnshops had done business with a David Stone from Fresno. Also, they checked with all coin dealers in the Central Valley and became aware of two transactions in which David Stone sold large quantities of gold and silver.

The first transaction took place in two phases and happened between the Bibee and Moyer murders. He sold silver bars to the Modesto Coin Shop in Modesto, California, which is approximately a one-hour drive from Fresno. One sale was on September 21, 1979, and the other was three days later.

They were informed by Detective Harry Scott from the Bakersfield Police Department of a second transaction. He told them that the Bakersfield Coin Shop may have done business recently with a David Stone. In mid-April, Wittman and McGowen contacted the shop's proprietors, Mike Becham and Larry Shallock. They identified a photograph of David Stone as a person with whom they had conducted a transaction that started with a telephone call on October 11, 1979, five days after the Moyer homicide. Although Stone had telephoned their shop several times during September 1979, they had their first personal contact with him a few days after October 11 when he came to their shop. Larry Shallock told the detectives that Stone said he had inherited a large quantity of gold and silver from his father, who had just died. The transaction consisted of Stone selling several thousand dollars' worth of gold and silver coins, as well as several silver bars, for which he was paid in cash, at his insistence.

Convinced that they were making progress, Wittman and McGowen decided to drive to Fresno to "snoop around—maybe rattle the doughboy's cage and see what happens." After having been informed by Detective Snow that the Stones had just recently moved from the residence on Backer Street, they ascertained the name of the owner of the residence. McGowen determined that the owner lived in Los Angeles and that her brother in Fresno was the caretaker. He contacted the brother, Juan Rincon, and was told that the Stones had moved out that week and he would be cleaning the house on Tuesday, April 29, to prepare it for renting. He agreed to allow the detectives to search the house before he cleaned it.

Wittman and McGowen met Detectives Snow and Reynolds at the Backer Street residence that Tuesday. Mr. Rincon was already there working in the yard and allowed them free access to the house. Upon entry, they found that all the furniture and personal items had been removed. All that was left were some empty boxes in the garage and a few items of trash found in the closet areas. Detective Reynolds found a spent .380-caliber casing and a live .22-caliber round on the floor of a hallway closet. The house was built on a raised foundation, and inside this hallway closet was a carpeted cover that, when removed, allowed entry into the space under the house. The two rounds found by Reynolds were lying adjacent to this cover.

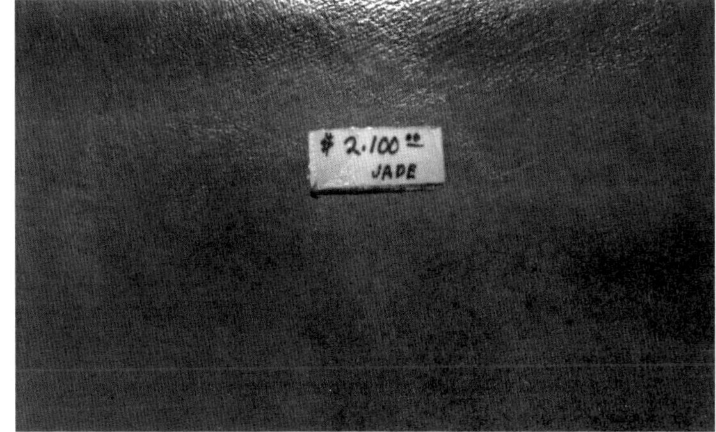

Homemade price tag found under David Stone's house. *Courtesy of Fresno Police Department.*

Wittman, remembering that the autopsy report on James Bibee indicated the body had likely been kept in a cool location prior to being found in the vehicle trunk, volunteered to crawl under the house and have a look. They removed the carpeted cover, and Wittman maneuvered himself into the opening. The space under the house was about three feet in height, and the only way to maneuver was to crawl on one's stomach.

Wittman lowered himself through the opening and lay down on his stomach. Although he used his flashlight, his view was limited because of the darkness and the confining space. About all that he could make out were the usual floor joists, cobwebs and spiders; however, one thing did catch his eye. From where he was lying, there appeared to be what he later described as "drag marks" leading away from his location that appeared to him to have been made by someone crawling along on his stomach—or by dragging something.

Crawling through the dirt, he followed these marks to their end about ten feet from the crawl space opening and shined his flashlight around. Lying within an arm's reach from him, he found a white button that appeared to be from a man's white shirt. He continued to move the beam of the flashlight around looking about him. Then he noticed something else that caught his attention. There in the dirt and darkness in the crawl space under a house on Backer Street in Fresno, California, some six months after the murder of Alex Moyer, he spotted a small item that would be that "one more piece of evidence" that would serve to convict David Stone of the murder of Alex Moyer. The item was a small piece of paper measuring approximately one inch in length by one-half inch in width. On the paper was printed "$2100 JADE." The small piece of paper was covered by transparent scotch tape.

Finding nothing else under the house, Wittman retrieved the button and the piece of paper, maneuvered his way back to the crawl space opening and climbed back into the house. "It looks like some sorta price tag," remarked Wittman as he showed his findings to the other detectives.

"Looks as though our little friend was hiding some things under the house," commented Gary Snow. "I wonder if he might have had Bibee's body under there."

Part IV
THE PROSECUTION

Murder Charges Filed

I did not meet Sergeant Bill Wittman until some four months after my arrival in Visalia. On a Monday morning, October 20, 1980, I was at my desk reading over police reports from the weekend that had been submitted for criminal filings when Wittman, along with Bill McGowen, appeared at my office door. "Hi, I'm Sergeant Wittman from VPD and this here's my partner Bill McGowen," he said as he strode forward, hand outstretched. I stood up, shook hands with both and asked what I could do for them.

"We got this little ol' murder case we're tryin' to file. We arrested the guy Thursday. I wonder if we could talk to you about it," Wittman responded. I asked them to sit down, and Wittman proceeded to inform me that the murder had occurred one year earlier and the case had been rejected several times by the District Attorney's Office. He then handed me an accordion folder of reports about four inches thick and explained that the suspect also killed someone in Fresno, but the Fresno County District Attorney's Office would not file on that case.

I was advised that on the previous Thursday, David Stone and his wife had stopped by the Visalia Police Department to pick up some items that had been seized when a search warrant was served on their residence by the Visalia and Fresno police in late March. Nothing of any evidentiary value resulted from the search, although Wittman did seize a few old presidential campaign buttons to show to Frank Moyer to possibly link them to his son's coin shop. When Mr. Moyer could not identify them, Wittman called Stone and told him to come after them. It was more of an act of frustration that prompted Stone's arrest. Upon arrival, he came sauntering into the police station threatening to "call his lawyer and sue everyone in sight" if they did not respond promptly and return his property. As Wittman said, "I had probable cause to arrest the little creep, so I just took another shot at gettin' a statement from him."

California law requires that anyone in custody be arraigned within forty-eight hours after an arrest, excluding weekend days and court holidays, or they must be released. This meant that because Stone had been arrested the previous Thursday, any charges against him had to be filed and he had to be arraigned that next Monday. I was not in a position to fully analyze the case in that short amount of time and convinced Wittman and McGowen that since Stone was not going to disappear on us, there was no harm in releasing him at this time. In addition, they informed me that the jewelry store robbery case was set for trial in January 1981. I indicated that I would read over the case and get with them later to discuss it. They agreed, and we made arrangements to meet later that week.

One of the joys of being a prosecutor is that, on occasion, you come across a case where you know the suspect is guilty but the evidence available to prove guilt is sparse. These types of cases are fascinating because they are like a good mystery and present a challenge to the prosecutor. Winning is always a good feeling, but winning when the odds are against you makes it even more satisfying. After reading all the available reports, I was totally convinced that David Stone was the one responsible for not only the murder of Alex Moyer but also the murder of James Bibee. Tulare County had jurisdiction only over the Moyer case, and I was resolved to convict David Stone of that crime.

Because there was no evidence that Stone had ever been in Tulare County, let alone Visalia, this was the classic circumstantial evidence case and had to be pursued in that manner. Ironically, the major piece of circumstantial evidence available was the Bibee murder. Whether Fresno County prosecuted that case or not, if I could get the court to allow the facts of that homicide into evidence in the Moyer case, I would have strong circumstantial evidence of the identity of Moyer's killer.

In California, there is a provision in the Evidence Code whereby evidence of another criminal act by a defendant may be presented to prove motive, intent, absence of mistake, method of operation (modus operandi) and identity. To be admissible, the other criminal act must have distinctively unique similarities to the criminal act in question. This provision applies whether the other criminal act was prosecuted or not, thus the fact that Fresno County did not choose to file the Bibee homicide did not affect my use of that evidence. I only had to convince the court that it was relevant and admissible.

In my view, there were such distinctively unique similarities between the two murders. Both victims made their living as self-employed dealers in gold and silver coins, which in itself was not a common occupation. They were both murdered after keeping an appointment with a person who purportedly wanted to engage in a coin transaction—that person being David Stone in the Bibee murder and, presumptively, a "David" from Fresno in the Moyer homicide.

Additionally, there were several other shared similarities. Both victims were extremely cautious and security-conscious and were killed without any sign of a struggle, indicating that they were taken by surprise. Each was shot numerous times from close range with a .22-caliber weapon. Both were robbed of only their most valuable gold and silver, with the assailant either disregarding or disposing of the less valuable items. The crimes occurred in cities within less than a one-hour drive of each other and occurred within two months of each other. It was to be my argument to the court that this was sufficient evidence to suggest that the same person was responsible for both homicides and, thus, the Bibee killing was relevant to show the assailant's identity in the Moyer case.

As agreed, I met with Wittman and McGowen and told them I would file the case against David Stone. However, there was one matter that I did not want to interrupt: Stone's robbery trial, scheduled for January, some three months away. I had contacted Deputy District Attorney Mike Idiart in Fresno, who was prosecuting the robbery case, and was assured by him that the trial, which had already been continued a few times, would take place as scheduled. He also asked me not to file the Moyer homicide until after the robbery trial so as not to give the defense a possible excuse to again continue it. I assured him I would hold off filing until January.

Both Visalia detectives were pleased that a filing was finally going to take place after all their months of work and agreed to follow up on some loose ends before January. One loose end that had not been resolved was the origin of the small piece of paper that appeared to be a price tag found under the Backer Street house. Bill Wittman was unable to find anyone to verify what it was. Tom Duffy was dead. The stress of her husband's murder had caused

Nell Bibee to suffer a stroke, and she was unable to give any meaningful information. Les Normart could not identify it, although he did think that it "looked like something Jim Bibee would have placed on an item to sell."

A few months later, Bill Wittman's perseverance paid off. He was able to locate one of James Bibee's friends, Harold Kelley, the same individual who had told Detective Snow that he was present in Tom Duffy's shop that fateful day of August 2. He had arrived just as David Stone and James Bibee were concluding their conversation. He was still present later when David Stone called and made arrangements with Bibee to come to the Stone house that afternoon to engage in a coin transaction. Kelley went over with Wittman what he remembered about the events of that August day and concluded by saying, "I never trusted that little guy. He'd come around talkin' like some sorta big shot, always tellin' tall stories 'bout how he was doin' this an' that. I thought him to be a liar and a blow-hard."

In recounting the events of that afternoon, Kelley related two things that particularly caught Wittman's attention. The first was that Stone had to give Bibee directions on how to get to his house. This totally contradicted both Stone's and his wife's assertions that Bibee had often come to the Stone residence to conduct transactions and, in fact, had been there just a month before the August meeting. Secondly, Kelley said that he overheard Stone boasting that his father had recently passed away and left him a large quantity of gold and silver coins. This was the same story he had told the people at the Bakersfield Coin Shop when he sold coins and silver bars some five days after the murder of Alex Moyer.

Wittman then pulled a small manila envelope from his file folder and said, "Mr. Kelley I want you to take a look at somethin'." He extracted the small piece of paper from the envelope and, showing it to Kelley, asked, "Do you recognize this?"

Harold Kelley took the item in his hand and unhesitatingly responded, "Yeah, I put this on a piece of jade that I had sold to Jim. He bought it from me and was goin' to resell it, but didn't know how much to ask. I told him to ask twenty-one hundred. Hell, I sold it to him for somethin' like fourteen or fifteen hundred. I told him he may as well start high and come down."

"How can you be sure this is the tag?" asked Wittman.

"Because I made this tag that day—that's my writing. I taped it to the box that the jade was in and helped Jim load it into the trunk of his car when he left Duffys' that evening."

"Thank you Mr. Kelley," said Wittman. "You've been a big help."

The Suspect

The jewelry store robbery case went to trial in Fresno as scheduled on January 12, 1981. As was becoming a pattern with events surrounding David Stone, the trial had a rather unusual twist, although it proceeded normally at first. The jury was selected, opening statements were made and evidence was presented. Stone presented an alibi defense and denied having committed the robbery. The evidence concluded on the morning of January 14. The court recessed for lunch, and final arguments were set to take place that afternoon. However, David Stone did not return to court. His bail was forfeited, and a warrant was issued for his arrest. He turned himself in the next day, whereupon both sides agreed to excuse the jury and submit the matter to the judge for decision. The judge found him guilty and set sentencing for February 13, 1981.

Once the conviction in Fresno occurred, I filed the case in Visalia charging David Stone with the robbery and murder of Frank Alexander Moyer Jr., also alleging that he used a firearm in commission of the offense. This allegation would add two years to his sentence should he be convicted of the murder and the allegation found true. Along with the complaint, a warrant was issued for the arrest of David Stone.

The Fresno court sentenced Stone to five years in prison. Four days later, Wittman and McGowen drove to the Fresno County Jail and had, as they explained it, "the pleasure of arresting the Doughboy and transporting him to Tulare County." Although he was sentenced to state prison, David Stone had a matter to take care of before he would actually make the trip to state prison. This matter was to last until May 1982, some sixteen months later, during which time David would be spending his days and nights in the Tulare County jail.

He was scheduled to appear for arraignment in the Visalia Municipal Court. In the meantime, I received a telephone call from attorney Jim Oliver indicating that he had been retained by the Stone family to represent David and wanted to pick up the police reports and agree on a date for the preliminary hearing. I had only been in Visalia for less than a year by this time and had not yet been involved in matters with all the local criminal defense attorneys. I had been told by other prosecutors and countless courthouse employees that Jim Oliver was one of the best criminal attorneys in the county, and I looked forward to handling this case against him.

We met in my office, and I found him to be a friendly, outgoing individual, a man who had been doing criminal defense work for as long as I had been an attorney—some thirteen years at this time. We discussed setting the preliminary hearing over several months to accommodate his schedule and give him more time to completely investigate the case, particularly since I told him that I intended to attempt to present the Bibee murder as evidence of identity. We picked a date and were scheduled to appear in court the next day for Stone's arraignment.

It was at the arraignment that I got my first look at David Stone. He was brought out of the custody cell wearing the jail clothing issued to all inmates. His hands were cuffed together, and the cuffs were fastened to a body chain around his waist. He was wearing leg chains, which prevented him from taking long strides, forcing him to shuffle as he walked. I was shocked at how young he looked. Although twenty-four years old at this time, he looked like a high school kid. He had a white, pasty look that all inmates soon acquire due to not being exposed to the outside. His hair was blond, and Wittman was right—he did look like the Pillsbury Doughboy. Short in stature, he had a pudgy, baby-fat look. He reminded me of the little guy who served as a water boy and handed out towels for the football team. A murderer was the last thing he looked like.

In what would soon become a regular occurrence whenever David was in court, both of his parents and his wife, Betsy, were present. Eston and Mary Stone were well dressed, pleasant-looking, middle-class people who one would not expect to have a son suspected of two murders. Indeed, their other three children were typical, normal, law-abiding people.

Mary Stone, in her late fifties, was a short, reserved mother of three boys and a girl; David was the third born. Eston Stone was a sixty-one-year-old retired control tower chief at Chandler Airfield in Fresno (it finally dawned on me several years later that his first name is his last name with a switch of the last letter *e* to the front). He was an outgoing person who, like his wife, absolutely refused to believe that David could kill someone. However, as I would find out later, he had some doubts about David's mental well-being and hired several psychiatrists and a private investigator to analyze and report on some of his son's bizarre activities that had never reached the stage of criminal prosecution.

Elizabeth Stone, known as Betsy, married David Stone in January 1977. They had a child who was two and a half years old at the time of David's arrest for murder, and Betsy was pregnant again. Blond and blue-eyed, she was an attractive woman in her early twenties and almost as tall as her husband. When Bill Wittman later contacted her parents, he determined that they were none too happy with the marriage. They inferred that Betsy could have done "much better," although in deference to their daughter, they would not come right out and say so directly.

The detectives involved in this case and I felt that she was the key player. She was purportedly present with David when he either met with or left for an appointment with both murder victims. We were split in our opinions—some felt she was an active participant who helped plan the crimes and supplied an alibi, but others felt that she knew what happened and was simply coerced by David to help supply an alibi. In either event, we determined that we should make a concentrated effort to get her to "roll over," as the law enforcement expression goes. There would be marital privileges as to testifying against one's spouse; however, if we could get her to tell us what *really* happened that Thursday evening and Saturday morning, we could deal with the privilege issue at a later time.

One approach we could use was arresting her (there certainly was probable cause to do so), granting her immunity and forcing her to give a statement. However, there would be no guarantee that any such statement would be other than a repeat of what we considered lies she had already told. Another option was to approach her by telling her we knew she had nothing to do with the murders and prevail upon her to do the right thing and tell the truth about what she knew.

We decided to try the latter approach. However, it soon became clear that Eston Stone and the rest of the Stone family must have been concerned about Betsy's vulnerability. They made it virtually impossible to contact her. With no source of income, a small child to raise and pregnant, she was supported by Eston Stone and his wife. She lived at their home and was totally dependent on them for her livelihood. As such, it seemed as though they monitored her every move. She could not be contacted by anyone from law enforcement without their being aware of it.

Bill Wittman had contacted Betsy's parents, who lived in the small town of Le Grand, several miles north of Fresno. In addition to showing their displeasure with the marriage, they inferred that they were also distrustful of David Stone. Although they had no direct evidence concerning either murder, Betsy's mother did make a curious statement regarding the day of the Bibee homicide, Thursday, August 2. She said that she thought Betsy had driven to Le Grand with the baby that day to visit her and Betsy's father, who had recently had surgery, and that she did not leave to return to Fresno until after dinner. When questioned further about the exactness of the date, she told Wittman that the child's birthday was the following day, August 3. Because they were unable to make it to the Stone's house for a birthday party that had been planned, Betsy agreed to come to Le Grand with the child the day before so they could have their own birthday party. The following day, August 3, was indeed the child's birthdate.

After being informed by Wittman that Betsy had told the police she was present when James Bibee came to the house that afternoon at 5:00 p.m., she suddenly and, as Wittman noted, "nervously" indicated that she "must have her dates mixed up about when Betsy visited." The clear impression received by Wittman was that upon realizing that what she said conflicted with her daughter's statements, she immediately became evasive and uncertain in an effort to protect her daughter. It appeared obvious that the mother suddenly became aware that her daughter, Betsy, had lied to the police to protect David and perhaps even herself as well. The answer to this question would be given by David Stone himself some three years and two trials later.

THE PRESENTATION OF EVIDENCE

The law in California provides that a felony case, such as murder, must first proceed through either a preliminary hearing or a grand jury proceeding. If the evidence presented meets the required standard of proof, the defendant will be held to answer for trial. The vast majority of cases go through the preliminary hearing procedure, and the hearing for the case of *The People v. David Stone* was scheduled for August 1981.

The standard of proof necessary at the preliminary hearing is different than the standard necessary at the trial stage. At the preliminary hearing, the prosecution need only present enough evidence to show that there is a reasonable suspicion that a crime has been committed and that the defendant committed same, whereas at the trial the prosecution must present evidence sufficient to prove the defendant guilty beyond a reasonable doubt. Because the standard of proof is so slight at the preliminary hearing, the prosecution will generally call just enough witnesses to meet this standard, and most often, the defense will call no witnesses. The reason the defense will normally not call any witnesses is because the prosecution's burden of proof is so slight that any defense witnesses' testimony would most likely not overcome this standard, and the defense may not want to reveal at this hearing what its defense might be at the trial stage.

There are times, however, when either side or both sides will call witnesses to testify at the preliminary hearing who might be unnecessary at the time, yet their availability for the trial later on might be open to some question. They may be in bad health and may not be able to testify later or they are transient and may not be able to be found when the trial time arrives. If a witness testifies at the preliminary hearing, and the other side has had an opportunity to cross-examine that witness, that testimony may then be used at the trial should the witness become unavailable. This is accomplished by reading the testimony from the preliminary hearing transcript as taken down by the court reporter.

It may also be important with reluctant or hostile witnesses to create a record of their testimony at the preliminary hearing before it changes to something different. Then, should their testimony at the trial differ in any respect, they can be confronted with the earlier testimony.

It appeared to me that it was imperative that I effectively put on all my available evidence at the preliminary hearing—that is, call all possible witnesses. This was because of the poor health of some, the possibility that some might leave the area and because my case was so circumstantial I felt that I needed to "test" it in the less scrutinizing setting of a preliminary hearing before the judge alone rather than in trial before a jury. In effect, this would serve as a dress rehearsal. This is not unusual in cases such as this, as Jim Oliver had indicated that he intended to call some witnesses in defense in the hope to convince the judge not to hold his client to answer. However, as we both knew, he wanted to preserve certain testimony should the matter go to trial. What this all promised was that the preliminary hearing would be a long one.

My first endeavor was to prepare a legal brief outlining my request to present evidence of the Bibee murder pursuant to California Evidence Code Section 1101(b). Unless I could convince the judge that this was relevant and admissible, my case against Stone for the Moyer murder was rather thin. I prepared the brief, filed it with the court and served the defense well before the preliminary hearing. The judge's decision whether to allow the Bibee evidence was to be decided about a week before the preliminary hearing. This was to allow both sides to adjust to whatever evidence was going to be admissible.

The case was set for the preliminary hearing in the Visalia Municipal Court of Judge Robert Van Auken. It should be noted that in 1981, the State of California had a two-tiered trial system, the Municipal Court and the Superior Court. In criminal matters, the Municipal Court heard preliminary hearings and misdemeanor cases; the Superior Court presided over all felony matters after a defendant had been held to answer for trial at the preliminary hearing. This was changed in 1994 when the two-tiered system was eliminated. Presently, there is only one trial court in California, the Superior Court, which hears all criminal matters, both misdemeanor and felony.

Judge Van Auken had come to Tulare County in the mid-1970s from the Los Angeles area. He worked in the Tulare County District Attorney's Office until he quit after some ill feelings developed between him and District Attorney Will Richmond. Van Auken then went to work for the Tulare County Public Defender's Office until he resigned and ran for municipal court judge.

Charles Flood was one of the two judges in the Visalia Municipal Court, and his position came up for election in June 1980. Van Auken sensed that Judge Flood was vulnerable due to some unpopular decisions he had made and because of his personal life. He left his wife and married a San Diego County judge whom he met at a judges' seminar. He apparently was commuting between San Diego and Visalia, the result being he was seldom on the bench. Van Auken seized on his vulnerability and borrowed money to finance a campaign to challenge Judge Flood. He organized a cadre of supporters to walk precincts, sought and obtained the support of many law enforcement agencies, posted campaign signs and generally devoted all his time and effort to winning the election. This effort, coupled with what was described as virtually no campaign at all by his opponent, enabled Van Auken to easily unseat Judge Flood.

Bob Van Auken was a small man, standing about five-foot-five and weighing no more than 125 pounds. Wearing thick glasses and of fair skin tone, he could almost have passed for a high school kid even though he was thirty-eight years old when I met him in June 1980, just after his election victory. He had a funny story he told that took place shortly after he took the bench in January 1981.

Van Auken liked to accompany police officers on patrol at night as a ride-along observer. This is something that many prosecutors do from time to time, and in fact, some prosecuting agencies encourage it. After Bob had assumed his duties as judge, he was riding one Saturday night with a Visalia Police Department officer when they responded to a disturbance call. There was a fight in a local bar that resulted in the police being summoned. After the dust cleared, several people were arrested for assorted offenses such as fighting, public drunkenness and disturbing the peace. Two rather large, biker-type individuals were handcuffed and placed in the back of the patrol car in which Bob was riding.

It was obvious to all that Bob was not a police officer since he was not wearing a uniform and carried no weapons; his smallish physical appearance was also not very reflective of the typical cop image. While riding to the station, the more vocal of the two men arrested, still in a mean mood and angry about being arrested, sized up Van Auken and asked, "Hey, little fucker, you wanna be a cop? You better grow up first. Does your mama know you're out? What Boy Scout troop are you in?" These taunts continued all the way to the station. Wisely, Van Auken didn't respond, and as it turned out, he didn't have to.

The following Monday afternoon, the prisoners in custody who were appearing for arraignment were led into the courtroom. Because the lockup was on one side of the courtroom and the jury box, which also served as prisoner seating, was on the other side, the prisoners had to walk across the courtroom directly in front of the judge. The bigmouth from Saturday night was among the prisoners. While walking across the courtroom to the jury box, he turned and looked directly into the smiling face of the judge—Robert Van Auken. As Bob told the story, the guy's face showed an expression of shock, his eyes got big and he gasped loud enough for all to hear, "Oh shit!"

The Moyer preliminary hearing was to be Judge Van Auken's first major case as a judge, and I was somewhat apprehensive about his decision in respect to the Bibee evidence, reasoning that he would want to take the safer way out because allowing evidence of an uncharged murder against a defendant required a decision of monumental importance.

Finally, the day of the motion arrived, and we argued for more than an hour before Judge Van Auken. I emphasized those authorities I had cited and compared the required criteria to the underlying facts in the Bibee and Moyer cases. The law requires that there be a balancing between the probative value of the evidence offered and its prejudicial effect. In essence, if the evidence sought to be admitted creates a prejudice to the defendant that outweighs its value as an item of proof, it is inadmissible. Jim Oliver argued that the Bibee evidence was excessively prejudicial and went beyond its worth as probative value. My argument was that the probative value outweighed the prejudicial effect because of the comparability between the two crimes, thus it was relevant in that it tended to show that the same person was responsible for both murders. The legal steps having been met, it was properly admissible for the trier of fact to consider on the identity issue, which of course was the sole issue in the Moyer case.

Judge Van Auken took the matter under submission and told us that he would render his decision the following morning. The next day, he ruled that the Bibee evidence would be admissible at the preliminary hearing. We were halfway home, and Wittman and McGowen were ecstatic. The ruling allowing the Bibee evidence would result in the preliminary hearing lasting much longer than it otherwise might have; however, that was fine with me. Because of Jim Oliver's schedule, other court business and the fact that we had to arrange the appearances of more than twenty-five witnesses, the hearing lasted one month.

The defense made a motion to have the preliminary hearing closed to the public and have all court records in respect to the case sealed. This was in an effort to ensure that should the case go to trial, the publicity would not interfere with the ability to pick a jury that would not have prejudged the case. Because this case was not only well publicized but also had the intriguing aspect of a second murder being offered as circumstantial evidence, the judge agreed with the defense request and closed the hearing. Much to my surprise, the closing of the hearing to the public went unchallenged by the press. Had it been challenged, there would have been a hearing on the issue before the judge.

The immediate family of the defendant were allowed to be in the courtroom, as was my wife, Charlotte. She was also intrigued by this case and on occasion would get the opportunity to watch a particular witness whose testimony promised to be important. No contact took place between Charlotte and the Stone family except for one brief exchange. During a recess, as she walked into the hallway outside the courtroom, Mary Stone said to her, "Why is your husband doing this to our son?" She responded, "Because he thinks he's guilty."

Oftentimes, the best way to assess the strength or weakness of a given case is not to rely on either the attorneys or the police officers who may be present in court, but rather to inquire of the court support staff what they think of the case. The participants are so close to the matter that their view of the evidence and evaluation of the witnesses may be skewed, whereas the court personnel know nothing about the case at the outset, hear it fresh and form those instinctive evaluations that jurors might well form. I always found it helpful to inquire of the court clerk, the court reporter and the bailiff what they thought of certain evidence or a given witness.

Judge Van Auken's clerk was a young woman named Kathy Gowin, married to a police officer for the City of Tulare. She had been a clerk for just over three years. The court reporter was a woman of approximately the same age named Annette Moore. Married to a court reporter for another judge in the Tulare County Municipal Court, she had been reporting for nearly seven years.

Several days into the preliminary hearing, as we broke for the day and after the defendant and his lawyer left the courtroom, I asked both of them their impressions of the case. They both related the same thing to me, saying that when they first saw David Stone, they could not believe that he could possibly be charged with murder, that he "looked like a choir boy in junior high school." However, after listening to the evidence and particularly after watching his reactions to some of the testimony, they were sure that he was responsible for both murders.

What they were referring to was David's apparently unconscious and uncontrollable habit of noticeably blinking whenever certain testimony was given. I was aware of this habit, but being unable to watch him closely while I was questioning the witnesses, I did not notice it. Both Kathy and Annette commented on it, saying that "it was creepy" and was most noticeable when the witnesses were describing finding James Bibee's body in the trunk of his car.

Their impression was that this nervous blinking occurred whenever the testimony reflected on the actual killings, such as the finding of the victims and the autopsy. In their opinions, this showed his guilty conscience. It was something I would want to exploit at trial.

The testimony of all the witnesses went pretty much as expected. In respect to the Moyer evidence, I was able to establish through Fred Sciacca and Henry Lawson that Alex Moyer had a large quantity of gold and silver coins on Tuesday that he was willing to sell. On Wednesday, he would not sell until he met with a prospective buyer from Fresno on Friday. The Friday meeting was later changed to Saturday. The telephone calls from Stone's residence to Moyer's shop corresponded with the time that the prospective buyer from Fresno contacted Moyer to set up the meeting and later to change the meeting from Friday to Saturday.

Frank Moyer Sr. testified that an inventory of the shop showed that there was very little gold and silver, thus the presumption that the killer took what was there. The physical evidence also showed no forced entry or sign of a struggle. The inference raised was that Moyer was in the midst of a transaction with a customer, most likely the buyer from Fresno, had the coins on the countertop and was suddenly taken by surprise and gunned down. In fact, my contention was that Moyer, when suddenly confronted by the customer pulling the gun, was reaching into the drawer under the countertop to pull his own gun when he was shot. A handgun was found, fully loaded, in a holster in the partially open drawer.

The physical facts also indicated that the killer used the key that Moyer always kept in the deadbolt lock on the inside of the door to unlock the door and then closed the door as he left and locked the deadbolt from the outside. The killer then took the key with him when he left the scene.

Two major issues presented themselves in respect to the Moyer murder. First, I had to identify the customer with whom Alex Moyer had the business appointment that was changed from Friday to Saturday morning. This was to be done through those persons who had contact with the victim the week before the murder and the telephone records.

Second, since all my circumstantial evidence showed that David Stone was that customer, I had to establish a time frame within which he could have committed the murder. The key witness to establish that time frame was a U.S. Postal employee named Joe Diaz. His testimony was crucial based on his knowledge of Moyer and the timing involved in his postal route.

In October 1979, Mr. Diaz had been delivering mail on the route that included the U.S. Stamp and Coin Shop for more than three years and knew Alex Moyer. On Saturday morning, his route would have him deliver mail at the coin shop around 10:45 a.m., give or take a few minutes. His usual routine, if Moyer's Cadillac was parked there and the lights were on in the coin shop, was to knock on the door and, upon Alex answering the door, exchange greetings and hand him the mail.

On Saturday morning, October 6, 1979, Joe Diaz observed Moyer's Cadillac parked in the parking area and the shop lights on. As was his custom, he knocked on the door; however, there was no answer, so he left the mail and went on about his route. He said that this occurred between 10:40 a.m. and 10:45 a.m. Diaz also testified that this routine of knocking on the door, Moyer answering and their exchanging greetings while being handed the mail happened virtually every Saturday; however, the events of that Saturday were highly unusual.

He also said something in passing that caught my attention. According to Diaz, on that Saturday morning, Moyer's Cadillac was not parked in the normal location. "It was very unusual for him to park his car that way," he told us as he described the location of the Cadillac depicted in a photograph taken on Sunday, the day after the murder. The testimony about the Cadillac's unusual location was the same as given by Lester Morris. Diaz then pointed out on the photograph the usual location where Moyer would park the car. This normal location was a space between the west side of the building and the curb along Dudley Street.

Because neither Diaz nor anyone else in the area of the coin shop saw Alex Moyer that morning, plus the fact that his car remained in the same location and the shop lights remained on, it was my contention that the only logical inference was that Alex Moyer was killed before Joe Diaz arrived on his mail route. There could be no other explanation. That being the case, I had to fit the murder between the time Alex Moyer was sighted by Dennis Gimlin driving past Early California Foods and the time David Stone and his wife checked out of the Fresno motel.

Other than the killer, Dennis Gimlin was the last known person to see Alex Moyer alive. His best estimate was that Moyer drove by his place of employment and honked and waved at him between 9:30 a.m. and 10:00 a.m. that Saturday morning. All of Moyer's customers and acquaintances said that he was a very punctual man, and his habit was to open his shop at 10:00 a.m. The drive from where Moyer waved at Dennis Gimlin to the coin shop took between fifteen and twenty minutes. Considering Gimlin's observations and Moyer's reputation for being punctual, it would be reasonable to conclude that he reached the shop at or just before 10:00 a.m., give or take a few minutes.

This being the case, David Stone would have met him there at 10:00 a.m. My contention was that Stone arrived first and parked in Moyer's normal parking location along the side of his shop. This was based on Lester Morris's and Joe Diaz's assertions that Moyer's Cadillac was not parked in his "usual parking place," thus forcing him to park his Cadillac where depicted in the photograph.

After entering the coin shop together, Moyer most likely locked the deadbolt from the inside and left the key in the lock, as was his normal procedure. Moyer then went behind the counter and placed the gold coins to be sold on the countertop, whereupon Stone pulled a gun. This prompted Moyer to attempt to open the drawer under the counter to pull his own handgun. Stone shot and killed Moyer. He then grabbed the coins on the countertop, not taking the time to take anything else, and exited, locking the door as he left and taking the key with him. Stone then drove to Fresno in time to check out of the motel at 10:58 a.m. The drive from the coin shop to Fresno on a Saturday morning would have taken between thirty and forty-five minutes depending on one's driving speed. This time frame would easily fit.

The only problem I foresaw in any scenario was that it appeared that someone, most probably Moyer, had brewed some coffee and poured at least one cup. This was because the coffeemaker was in the "on" position, according to McGowen's report of the crime scene. Coffee residue was in the pot, and a half-full cup of coffee was on the desk next to the counter. These facts became known as the famous "coffee pot evidence," which, two years later, would present a major issue. Based on the undeniable fact that this coffee was present when the body was discovered, I had to explain it in some manner, and it appeared there were three different explanations.

The first explanation was that Moyer brewed the coffee when he arrived that Saturday morning, poured a cup and drank some of it and then was killed by Stone. This explanation would present a tight fit within the time frame I was working with—to brew the coffee would cut into the time by several minutes. The residue left in the pot would be the result of it being in an "on" position, thus evaporating between that Saturday morning and Sunday when the crime was discovered.

The second explanation, and the one I felt several years later was the only logical one based on a later experiment, was that Moyer had made the coffee the day before and left it when he closed the shop on Friday. Therefore, what the police found that Sunday at the crime scene was Friday's coffee and residue left in the pot and in the half-full cup.

The third explanation was that the coffee was started sometime well after Moyer arrived that Saturday morning. The assertion, offered several years later, was that it had to have been started between 6:00 p.m. and 9:00 p.m. that Saturday evening.

Either of the first two explanations would still accommodate David Stone as being the killer, but obviously the third would not. At the preliminary hearing, the defense seemed to be setting the stage for some scientific evidence regarding the coffeepot and the residue left inside. Jim Oliver questioned McGowen extensively about what he found and what he put in his report of the crime scene.

I called Harold Kelley as a witness at the preliminary hearing for two reasons. First and foremost, he was the one who made the jade price tag found by Wittman under David Stone's house. He had affixed it to the box containing the jade figurine and placed the box in the trunk of Bibee's car the day he disappeared. This I considered the most important piece of physical evidence in the Moyer case, even though it pertained to the Bibee homicide. Second, Mr. Kelley was in poor health and suffering from a variety of ailments, most significant of which were emphysema and heart problems. My concern was that he might not be available to testify at trial, so I was intent on having a thorough and complete transcript of all that he could offer in respect to the Bibee case. As it turned out, he was able to testify at trial, although his health had deteriorated somewhat. Nevertheless, his later testimony was just as dramatic as it was at the preliminary hearing.

Harold Kelley's testimony was powerful, as he described in detail that he was familiar with David Stone and was present in Tom Duffy's shop that day in August when his good friend Jim Bibee made arrangements with Stone to go to Stone's house that evening to engage in a gold and silver coin transaction. He further testified that Bibee had indicated that David Stone said he had inherited a large amount of gold and silver and could not bring it into Duffy's shop to trade. He also testified to his familiarity with Bibee's business habits, that he did not customarily do business anywhere except at his rented space in Duffy's shop and that he had to receive directions on how to get to Stone's house.

He described the jade figurine and how he had sold it to his friend Bibee several weeks before, as well as Bibee's intention to resell it. He explained that it was his suggestion that the sale price be set at $2,100 and how he, Harold Kelley, made the price tag and taped it to the blue felt-covered box containing the figurine. In detail, he explained how Jim Bibee would transport his coins to and from Duffy's shop in a cardboard box that he

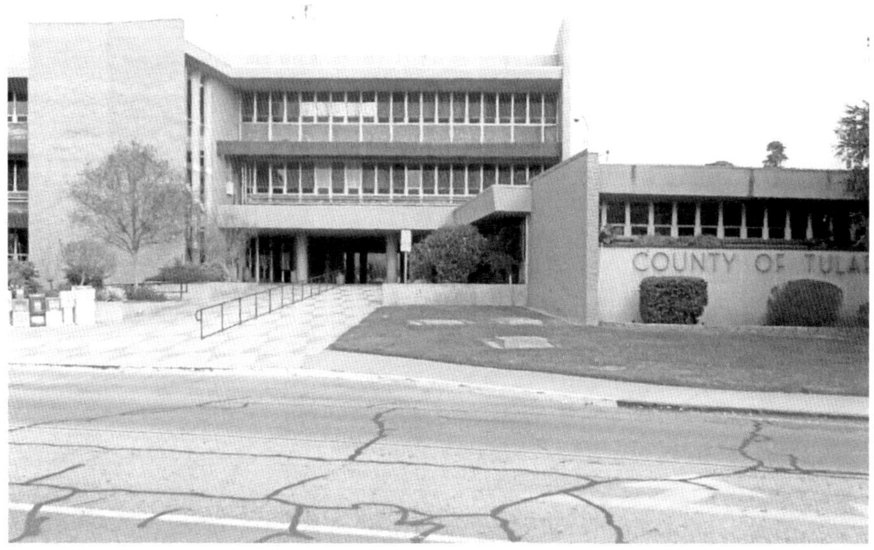

Tulare County Superior Court. *Courtesy of Ryan Bilbrey.*

Suspect in murder of coin dealer bound over after long hearing

The case file of the man accused of murdering coinshop dealer Frank Moyer has been sealed until Sept. 16.

On that date, the defendant, David Edward Stone, 23, will be arraigned in superior court on charges of murder and robbery in the 1979 slaying of Moyer, who was known to deal in gold.

Stone's attorney, James Oliver, said Monday that he would be requesting a "gag order" from the Superior Court to keep conversation about the case to a minimum before it comes to trial. It was at Oliver's request Monday that Visalia Municipal Court Judge Robert C. Van Auken ordered the case file sealed until Stone's arraignment.

Van Auken ordered Stone bound over to the Superior Court Monday, after a preliminary hearing that stretched out over a month's time and was closed to the public. The hearing included defense testimony, in addition to the prosecution witnesses called by Deputy District Attorney Ronn Couillard.

Oliver said Monday that he would ask for the "gag order" to prevent the possibility of a change of venue in the case.

Stone was arrested in Fresno in January by Visalia Police Agent Bill McGowan and Sgt. Bill Wittman after a 15-month investigation. Stone, at the time of his arrest, was awaiting sentencing for steaing at gunpoint more than $25,000 in diamonds from a Clovis jewelry store in 1978.

Coinshop dealer Moyer had lived in the Exeter area for 10 years, commuting to his Murrary Street shop, U.S. Stamp and Coin, where his body was discovered on Oct. 7, 1979. Puzzling aspects of the crime included the fact that the door to the shop was locked and firemen had to be called in to use heavy-duty saws to cut open the locking mechanism.

David Stone held to answer for Moyer homicide. *From the* Visalia Times-Delta.

always placed in the trunk of his old Chevrolet sedan. Then Mr. Kelley testified that the last time he saw Jim Bibee alive was when he, Kelley, helped his friend place the coin collection and the felt-covered box containing the jade figurine with the $2,100 price tag into the trunk of the Chevrolet sedan. This was about 4:00 p.m. to 4:30 p.m. on that fateful Thursday.

In all, I called twenty-six witnesses to testify at the preliminary hearing. After making statements to the effect that they would put on a full-blown defense, Jim Oliver presented only two witnesses, neither of whom testified to anything of substance. I had anticipated this, as it just did not seem to be good strategy to present a defense at this time. After both sides rested, Judge Van Auken took the case under submission before making a decision whether or not to hold Stone to answer for trial in the Superior Court.

I was confident that the evidence presented a reasonable suspicion that David Stone had been identified as the killer of Alex Moyer. However, Judge Van Auken was wavering in making that ruling, indicating that there was no evidence ever placing David Stone in Visalia. Finally, after much argument back and forth between Oliver and myself, the judge ruled that Stone would have to stand trial for the murder of Alex Moyer. He did, however, dismiss the robbery charge due to a lack of evidence. I could not complain about this dismissal because, in fact, there was only speculation in respect to any actual loss, even though robbery was the motive behind the murder.

Wittman, McGowen and both Fresno detectives Snow and Reynolds were overjoyed and vowed to do whatever I needed to prepare for trial. I remember Detective Reynolds remarking, "I don't care if the little SOB has to fall on your case and not ours, just so we get him off the streets."

THE TRIAL

David Stone, represented by Jim Oliver, was arraigned in the Tulare County Superior Court for the Moyer murder. He pled not guilty, and trial was set for November 1981. In California, when a person has been held to answer for trial on a felony charge, that person has a right to be brought to trial within sixty days from the filing of the Information (this is the name of the charging document that is filed in the Superior Court). The November trial date was within that sixty-day period; however, I really did not expect the case to go to trial then.

When a person is charged with an extremely serious crime such as murder, it is not unusual for the trial to take place well after the sixty-day period. There are several reasons for this. The defense, until this time, has not normally concluded, or probably even started, its own investigation and thus needs additional time. Also, these cases will normally take longer to try, and the defense attorney may have to schedule a block of time for the trial, which will often be beyond the sixty days.

Nevertheless, in order not to be caught short, Wittman and McGowen immediately started to look for new leads in the case. Even though a given case may be set for trial, the investigative work does not necessarily end. Follow-up contacts are made with certain witnesses to ascertain whether they can recall something that may have been missed earlier, and there is a continual search for additional witnesses and evidence.

No murder weapon had been located for either the Moyer or Bibee murders. However, we did have ballistic evidence that both were killed by a .22-caliber weapon, although it was not the same .22-caliber weapon. We also had evidence that David Stone was something of a gun enthusiast. He had access to guns, keeping one in his home and another under the front seat of his car. He also had worked for a brief period at Herb Bauers

Sporting Goods in Fresno, where other employees described him as being very knowledgeable about firearms.

Additionally, we had information that David's father, Eston Stone, had a concealed weapons permit and that one of the guns listed in the permit was a .22-caliber handgun. Immediately after the preliminary hearing, a search warrant to search the home of Eston Stone in Fresno for the weapon listed on the weapons permit was drafted and presented to a judge for authorization. The judge signed the warrant, and Wittman and other Visalia police officers executed that warrant in September 1981.

They found several weapons at the Stone residence but not the one listed on the concealed weapons permit. When questioned about this weapon, Eston Stone told Wittman and the other officers that it had been stolen from his daughter-in-law Betsy's car several years before. As it eventually turned out, at trial he contradicted Wittman's testimony and that of another officer, saying that the gun had been loaned to his daughter, Holly, and was stolen from *her* car, not from the car of his daughter-in-law Betsy, David's wife. He said that when informed of the theft, he had reported it stolen to the Clovis Police Department.

Bill Wittman contacted the Clovis Police Department regarding a report of a stolen gun by Eston Stone. He determined that on October 16, 1979, Eston Stone had reported this particular weapon stolen. The information was received by a dispatcher and placed on a card kept in the police department files. The card revealed that Mr. Stone told them the .22-caliber firearm was stolen from *his* car while it was parked in front of the Straw Hat Pizza at noon. Most curious was the date of the theft: Friday, October 5, 1979—the day before the Moyer murder. Things were getting most interesting.

It seems that Eston Stone was understandably concerned about whose car the gun was stolen from, by testifying at trial that it was taken from his daughter Holly's car rather than from the car driven by Betsy. We knew that the car David and Betsy drove at that time was owned by Eston Stone, thus the information given to the Clovis Police about it being stolen from Holly's car was highly suspicious.

As we had all thought, Jim Oliver made a motion to continue the trial from November to after the first of the year, citing the need for further investigation and his own scheduling difficulties. I had no problem with a short continuance and agreed. The case was set for March 22, 1982, in the court of Judge Edward Kim.

Judge Van Auken's ruling to allow the Bibee evidence to be used at the preliminary hearing did not necessarily bind the trial court to allow it at trial. This meant that the issue of admissibility of the Bibee evidence would be ruled on by Judge Kim. I decided to file my motion well before trial to alert the judge that there was this other potential evidence. Jim Oliver filed his response to my motion, and Judge Kim indicated that he would read the motions and hear argument during the trial. This would not allow me to discuss Stone's involvement in the Bibee murder during opening statement. It also gave a degree of uncertainty to both the prosecution and the defense in preparing for trial.

One thing that a prosecutor is never sure of when trying a criminal case is whether the defendant will testify on his own behalf. The law states that a defendant in a criminal action has the right not to be compelled to testify. Therefore, unlike for a civil case, the prosecutor in a criminal case cannot call the defendant as a witness. The decision whether to testify lies solely with the defendant and his attorney. Many considerations go into the decision: whether the defendant would be a good witness, can express himself adequately, is likely to become flustered and look bad on the witness stand or is likely to do poorly upon being vigorously cross-examined by the prosecutor; whether there are certain things that he simply cannot explain adequately; and whether he has a prior criminal conviction with which he can be impeached. The defense may feel that it can sufficiently defend the case without the defendant testifying. If the defendant does not testify, the jury is instructed by the court that the fact he has not testified cannot be considered by the jury in arriving at a verdict.

I felt that David Stone would testify. My thoughts were that although he had a prior robbery conviction that could be used to impeach his testimony and though the evidence of the Bibee case presented a major problem to explain, he would testify nevertheless. Impeachment means that on the issue of credibility, the jury may consider the fact that the witness has a prior felony conviction (i.e., is he truthful). In my experience, impeachment with a prior conviction, be it of the defendant or any other witness, is vastly overrated. The witness defuses the effect by admitting to the prior conviction when he first takes the witness stand, and thus it is out of the way and the focus turns to what the witness has to say about the case at hand. In my opinion, prosecutors get too excited over a defendant's prior convictions.

The Bibee case presented a much more serious matter. Oliver could, however, always rely on the fact that the Bibee murder was more than two years old and the Fresno authorities did not see fit to charge Stone. This could conceivably defuse its effect. I felt that the explanation of his activities the day Moyer was killed, something that I could not refute, and the tight time frame within which I had to fit the crime would present a strong possibility that he would take the witness stand. Also, from discussing the personality of David Stone with the investigators, it was evident that he thought he was smarter and cleverer than the investigators, thus the feeling was that he thought he could convince the jury that he was not guilty.

In order to be better prepared to cross-examine, I made an effort to get some insight into the personality of Mr. David Stone. To do this, I had access to reports forwarded to me by Mike Idiart, the deputy district attorney who prosecuted David for the jewelry store robbery in Fresno. These consisted of Fresno Police Department reports and medical reports that had been prepared regarding David's mental condition. One such report had been prepared by, of all persons, David's father, Eston Stone. Additionally, I had several tapes of conversations between David and Fresno detectives. What I found out revealed a series of bizarre and unusual events that started in June 1978 and continued right up through the time of the Moyer murder.

It seems that David Stone was the suspect in several theft-related incidents that had been investigated by the Fresno Police Department before the Bibee murder. However, he was never prosecuted on any of these. The first was when David was employed as a bank teller at Crocker Bank in Fresno. On June 1, 1978, a $6,000 shortage was found, and based on the circumstances, David Stone was the prime suspect. When confronted with the charge, he denied it; however, he was fired from his position. Apparently, the evidence was insufficient to pursue a criminal charge.

The second incident occurred some five months after the December 28, 1978 jewelry store robbery for which he had not, as yet, been arrested. This involved a convoluted series of strange events. David had a job driving a Federal Express van making deliveries. At that time, the Federal Express headquarters was located at the Fresno Air Terminal. On May 23, 1979, at approximately 11:00 a.m. while making a delivery, David reported his van stolen. Soon after the report, the van was recovered by the Fresno police, whereupon David and his supervisor, Bill Harrington, went to the Fresno station to obtain the van. It appeared that nothing had been stolen from the van. This was at approximately 1:30 p.m.

At 2:30 p.m., David was assigned to deliver two packages and left headquarters. The procedure for delivery drivers was to report in every thirty minutes. David did not report in until 6:00 p.m., according to supervisor Harrington.

In the meantime, David went to Boot's Camera, a retail camera store in Fresno, and purchased some camera equipment totaling $2,249.70. He gave the sales clerk an involved story about going to South Africa with three friends for a film production concerning South Africa's economic impact on free-world nations. According to a written report by Eston Stone, David had supposedly been in contact with a Frank Land of the South African Information Office in Los Angeles regarding such a project. One of the sales clerks to whom he was telling this story recognized David from high school. He paid for the equipment with a starter check from Lloyd's Bank in Fresno. This purchase occurred on Wednesday, May 23, 1979, at approximately 4:30 p.m. When David returned to Federal Express at 6:00 p.m., he showed the camera equipment to Bill Harrington and another employee.

The next day, May 24, at 9:15 a.m., David appeared in the Lloyd's Bank and withdrew $200, which left the account virtually empty. Later that morning, an employee from Boot's Camera came to the bank and attempted to acquire a cashier's check against David Stone's account for the amount of the check that had been written for the camera equipment the day before. The request could not be honored due to David's withdrawal less than an hour earlier.

The bank, assuming that someone may have stolen one of David's checks and made the camera purchases, telephoned him and questioned him regarding his checks being stolen and his desire to sign a forgery complaint. At first, he did not want to sign one, but then he changed his mind and said he would do so. That afternoon, David came to the bank to sign the forgery complaint, and just as would occur later with the victim of the jewelry store robbery, he came face to face with an employee of Boot's Camera who had gone to the bank to ascertain why the check would not clear. The employee recognized David and confronted him about the check. David asserted that it was not his. He left the bank without signing the forgery complaint. Eventually, Eston Stone paid off the camera store, and charges were never filed. The camera equipment was never found.

The next day, May 25, David resigned his position at Federal Express without a reason and without giving notice.

Included in the report written by Eston Stone about his son's strange actions was an incident a few weeks after the Boot's Camera encounter. Apparently, David told his family that on June 5 he was going to Los Angeles to meet with Frank Land of the South African Information Office. Later that day, Mr. Stone received a telephone call from David during which he claimed that he was robbed in the restroom at the Los Angeles International

Airport. Claiming that one could be robbed in such a crowded location as a restroom at LAX seemed highly suspicious. A report was allegedly made; however, Wittman could never verify any such report. We always suspected that David made this claim to cover up some illegal activity but could never determine what it may have been.

In March 1980, David reported a burglary of his home. He stated that upon returning to his home after being gone for several hours, he found the home had been entered and many items were missing. He filed a claim with the insurance company to be reimbursed for the losses incurred. The police and the insurance company both began to investigate, and just as with so many other activities where David Stone was involved, things did not appear normal. There was no sign of a forced entry, and the neighbors reported seeing nothing unusual. David's time frame varied with each story he told the police, and in total, the whole incident appeared to be a hoax. They were soon to discover that David had rented a space at a local mini-storage. Upon searching it, they found all the purportedly missing items. Again, no criminal charges were ever filed.

It was also evident that the more he was allowed to talk, the more he tended to exaggerate and focus attention on himself. An example of this was a story he told Fresno police officers about his short sojourn in the U.S. Navy. It seems that right out of high school, he joined the navy and was sent to boot camp in San Diego. He never made it through boot camp, eventually receiving a medical discharge due to his unfitness both physically and emotionally for military duty. However, his explanation for the discharge was somewhat bizarre.

In a taped interview, he told the police officers that while at boot camp, he was detailed with several other recruits to clean the barracks floor. They were supposedly given a liquid cleaning compound that they poured on the floor. Shortly thereafter, while mopping, they were all overcome by poisonous fumes from the cleaning compound. He claims that he lost consciousness and memory and was hospitalized for several days. Based on this poisoning, the navy gave him a medical discharge so that no more would come of the incident and it could "hush it up."

Attempts to verify this story were made. The Fresno police detectives at that early time in the Bibee investigation thought that perhaps David Stone might have some mental problems based on all the strange activities that were linked to him. They thought he could be doing some of these things and not remembering afterward. The navy poisoning story fit in with this scenario. However, the navy could not verify the story, there were no records of David Stone being in the hospital and no reported incidents of any "poisonings" at the navy recruit training base. Once again, it was another wild story concocted by David Stone to give a flair to something and gain attention to himself.

The medical reports that had been prepared in an effort to explain some of these unusual behavior patterns indicated that David was not suffering from any mental disorders. They did point out, however, that he was "over-talkative," rather expressive and dramatic, quite spontaneous and somewhat paranoid about the Fresno Police Department's "attempt to get him for the Bibee murder." One report added that "he does an excessive amount of squinting which seems unconscious and uncontrollable, particularly when difficult areas are discussed."

After reading all the reports and listening to the taped interviews between David and the police, my thought was that he was his own worst enemy. His desire to talk and seemingly having an explanation for everything tended to lead to him rambling, self-contradicting and exaggerating to the extent that he appeared to be shading the truth. Added to that was the fact that his squinting would become noticeable when he talked about areas where he is most vulnerable, such as the Bibee visit, thus implying a consciousness of guilt.

Considering all of this, it seemed that if David Stone testified, the best approach in cross-examining him would not to be overly aggressive, but rather question him in a low-key manner. It was evident from his taped conversations with the police that this form of questioning gave him a stage to try to take control of any discussion. By doing so, he would be willing to talk freely. It also would provide him a forum to ramble, whereupon he would eventually give contradictory responses. As it eventually turned out, I was to try David Stone twice for the murder of Alex Moyer, and in one of those trials, I was able to use this technique, resulting in a rather disastrous admission on his part.

Judge Edward Kim had a reputation among trial attorneys as a judge who ran an efficient court. When matters were scheduled, he expected them to be heard on the date and at the time set. The same was true when a trial was being conducted in his court. He expected the witnesses to be present and called to the witness stand without any delays. He would get very upset and could be rather caustic when attorneys would waste time or be unprepared or when witnesses were not present. This could result in some embarrassment to the offending attorney in front of the jury. As a result, some attorneys did not like to try cases in front of Judge Kim; however, I did.

I appreciated the fact that he kept the trial moving. Some defense attorneys used the tactic of delay in a jury trial under the theory that the impact of a witness's testimony tends to diminish as time goes by, thus by extending the trial, the jury would not have as fresh a recollection of a given witness's testimony when they went into deliberations. Absent a valid emergency, these delays were not possible in Judge Kim's court.

The People of the State of California v. David Stone began on March 22, 1982. In the afternoon session, a large panel of potential jurors was summoned to Judge Kim's courtroom for jury selection. The selection process consists of questioning prospective jurors to determine their qualifications to sit as a trial juror—such as whether they have any knowledge of the case to the extent that they could not be fair. We also had to determine whether they could spend the estimated three to four weeks necessary to complete the case. Once these determinations have been made, the attorneys then have the opportunity to excuse any juror. This is called the peremptory challenge phase, and it continues until both sides have used up their allotted number of challenges or until both sides pass simultaneously.

This peremptory challenge phase usually turns into a cat-and-mouse game between the two sides. Most of the time, in any jury selection process, there are a few jurors the prosecution will want to excuse and several the defense will want to excuse, based solely on their demeanor and/or answers to the questions posed to them. Experienced attorneys know this and recognize that a juror who appears to be somewhat sympathetic to their case will most assuredly be excused by the opposing side. The experienced attorney will also recognize that when selecting a group of twelve people, the odds are that some of those twelve may not necessarily be favorable to their side, be it the prosecution or the defense. The reasons are they may dislike the defendant or the victim, they may dislike a particular witness presented or they may even tend to dislike the attorney. Therefore, the attorney wants to minimize this situation. This is obviously done by attempting to spot tell-tale signs of this dislike and excuse those jurors who tend to exhibit it. However, this recognition is difficult and not always possible. Thus, the attorney will try to select a core of one or two jurors with strong personalities and who appear not to have any of these latent dislikes. The theory is that during deliberation, the jurors with stronger personalities will prevail over those with meeker personalities and hopefully not allow the discussions to focus on any of these areas of dislike.

Jury selection is obviously an important aspect of a trial; however, it is also true that attorneys often tend to outsmart themselves in choosing a jury. Some attorneys will automatically excuse persons employed in (or those related to persons employed in) certain occupations. For example, prosecutors may excuse schoolteachers because they think they are too liberal and would be reluctant to vote guilty, or defense attorneys will always excuse persons related to police officers under the assumption they would always vote for guilt. I was never one to subscribe to these stereotypes, relying more on my gut reaction to the individual after listening and watching them answer the questions asked of them during the jury selection process.

One form of strategy that all attorneys engage in is to select a group of jurors based on the nature of the charges, the type of witnesses who will testify and the nature of the defendant. In this case, my concern was to select jurors strong enough to vote guilty. David Stone did not look like a person the typical juror would envision as a killer, and I was going to ask the jurors to find him guilty of a coldblooded murder. Thus, I wanted to be assured that the jurors would not be influenced by sympathy for David's family, all of whom I knew would be present throughout the trial, nor did I want them to be swayed by the innocent looks of this baby-faced defendant. One of the questions I asked of many jurors was that if they believed that I had proven David Stone guilty of murder, could they vote for guilt in the jury room and then return to the courtroom, and if asked, could they look at him and say that they had voted for guilt. Not only was I interested in their verbal response to this type of question, but I was also watching closely for their emotional and physical reaction (their body language) in answering the question. Did they exhibit conviction in their answer, or did they appear to waver?

It was readily apparent that Jim Oliver was seeking a jury made up of older, grandmotherly women who might feel that no young man as innocent-looking as David Stone could commit these vicious murders. One of my goals in jury selection was to try to avoid having this type of juror selected. I had no particular desire to get more men than women, or vice versa, but rather to excuse any potential juror whom I felt would be swayed by Stone's innocent appearance.

As was typical of Judge Kim's court, we went through jury selection in a rapid fashion, selecting a jury that afternoon. The jury consisted of seven women and five men, with two women as alternate jurors. In analyzing the jury, I felt that both Jim Oliver and I got the mixture of people, occupations and personalities that we both expected, with one exception. During the selection process, as jurors are excused by the attorneys, another prospective juror is called from the audience as a replacement. Toward the end of the selection process, a man named Herman Ziegler was called. A large athletic-looking man in his late fifties or early sixties, he gave his occupation as an assistant high school principal. Most interesting to me, he said that he was the one who handles disciplinary problems at the school. I recognized immediately that I wanted Mr. Ziegler on the jury, and when my opportunity came to ask him questions, I declined. For some reason, Oliver did not excuse him from the panel; he later told me that he thought that his background as the person in charge of discipline at the school would work in David's favor. Leaving Herman Ziegler on the jury assured both of us that he would form a strong and unwavering opinion.

When we started the trial, although I was somewhat uncertain whether David Stone would testify in his own behalf, I was rather certain that Betsy Stone would testify. In California, the spouse of one charged with a criminal offense has the right to refuse to testify against their spouse unless either they or their child is a victim of the crime, thus Betsy had the right not to testify if I called her as a witness. Because it is improper to force the spouse to exercise the privilege in the presence of the jury, I requested a hearing out of the jury's presence to determine the issue. I informed Jim Oliver that

Wednesday, March 24, 1982 Visalia Times-Delta — 1B

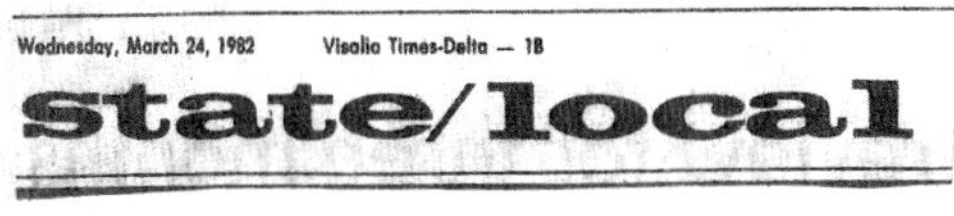

state/local

Moyer murder trial begins

According to the prosecution, David Edward Stone checked into a Fresno motel, just a few miles from his Clovis home, as an alibi, drove into Visalia early Saturday, Oct. 6, 1979, pumped five .22 caliber bullets into coin dealer Frank Alexander Moyer Jr., stole several thousand dollars worth of South African gold coins and returned to Fresno where he immediately checked out of his room.

Stone, 24, cashed the stolen Krugerrands in Bakersfield five days later, according to Deputy District Attorney Ronn Couillard.

That's the picture the prosecution painted to eight-woman, four-man jury Tuesday in its opening statement in the 2½-year-old murder case being heard in Tulare County Superior Court. Judge Edward Kim is presiding.

Stone's attorney, James Oliver, reserved his opening statement for later in the trial.

Moyer, 49, of Exeter was a careful, cautious man who was "very security-conscious," according to David Dye, a former employee. Moyer's store, U.S. Stamp and Coin at Murray Avenue and Dudley Street, wasn't a typical coin shop where people could just walk in off the streets, Dye testified. Moyer would only open the door for regular customers or people with whom he had appointments. After customers entered, he locked the door behind them. Moyer kept a loaded Browning .22 automatic in his desk and always kept a button nearby for triggering an alarm system.

But his killer got by all those precautions by apparently making an appointment to purchase his entire stock of gold that Saturday morning, Couillard alleged.

Couillard described the prosecution's view of events in the murder in order to give the jury a "word picture of where we are going." He said 20 to 25 witnesses are expected to be called during the trial, which is expected to last for several weeks.

One of the key factors in the trial will be establishing the time of death in order to prove that Stone had time to drive to Visalia and commit the murder about 10 a.m. and return to Fresno and check out of his motel by 10:58 a.m.

Problems with timing were mentioned by Municipal Court Judge Robert C. Van Auken when, in August, he came close to dismissing the case against Stone for lack of evidence, according to the transcript of the August preliminary hearing. That transcript, sealed until this week in accordance with a "gag order" from a Superior Court judge, reveals that Van Auken listed a series of what he considered problems in the prosecution's case.

"There is no recorded testimony of any person ever seeing the defendant, Stone, at or near the premises (of Moyer's shop), either before or after the alleged date of the homicide," Van Auken told the attorneys, according to the transcript.

While Van Auken eventually bound Stone over on the murder charge, he dismissed the special allegation of robbery — an allegation which could have resulted in a death sentence. Testimony during the trial Tuesday

(See MURDER, page 5B)

Murder case - - -

(Continued from page 1B)

indicated that an open safe, with $5,000 in cash visible in envelopes inside, was left at the scene of the slaying.

Moyer died of five bullet wounds to the chest and back, according to the testimony of pathologist John Morrison.

Moyer was last seen alive between 9 and 10 a.m. Saturday in Exeter as he drove to work, according to the prosecuting attorney. Couillard added that Moyer typically opened the shop about 10 a.m. on Saturdays and that a Visalia mailman received no answer when he knocked on the shop's door between 10:40 and 10:45 a.m. that Saturday. Moyer's body was not discovered until 8:30 a.m. Sunday when neighbor Dale Heslinga spotted the body through a window in the door and notified police.

Dye testified that Moyer often had several thousand dollars in gold Kruggerrands on hand and that the shop owner often scribbled phone messages for orders on a notepad by the phone.

A message left by Moyer's phone, allegedly in Moyer's handwriting, mentions the name "David" in reference to gold, Couillard said. Stone sold between $8,000 and $10,000 worth of gold and silver coins in Bakersfield five days after the murder, Couillard said in his opening statement.

Stone was arrested for the Moyer murder in January of 1981 in Fresno while he was awaiting sentencing for stealing at gunpoint more that $25,000 in diamonds from a Clovis jewelry store in 1978. His conviction is on appeal, according to Oliver.

Visalia Times-Delta, March 24, 1982.

I intended to subpoena Betsy as my witness. Based on that information, he had her state under oath that she was exercising her privilege not to testify as a prosecution witness. This did not, of course, prevent her from testifying for the defense.

In a casual conversation before trial, Jim Oliver intimated that he would call Betsy to testify, indicating he felt she would be a good witness and make a good impression on the jury. I had hoped he would, believing, as did all the detectives, that she was either directly involved or knew her husband was guilty, and based on some of the statements she made regarding the Bibee case, I thought that I could make some strong points in cross-examining her. She attended every day of trial until I rested my case, and then she failed to appear. I could sense from Oliver's reactions that he was upset. Her failure to testify reaffirmed our suspicions about her culpability and/or knowledge.

On Wednesday, March 24, after I had put on my evidence of the Moyer murder, Judge Kim heard argument on admission of the facts of the Bibee murder. He ruled that it could be offered as an uncharged criminal act. Judge Kim did, however, instruct the jury that the Bibee evidence could only be considered on the issue of identity of the person responsible for the Moyer homicide. I could sense how confused the jurors were when I began to offer evidence of a murder they had heard nothing about. It appeared to have a somewhat dramatic effect, if the looks on their faces were any indication.

In total, I called thirty witnesses, and the defense called seven. I was confident that the jury would be convinced that Alex Moyer was killed by the person he met on Saturday morning, October 6, 1979. The many contacts with the coin shop—postman Joe Diaz from 10:40 a.m. to 10:45 a.m., Lester Morris's presence in the adjoining office from 11:30 a.m. until 3:30 p.m. and the Heslingas' attempt to contact Moyer that evening—all strongly indicated that Alex Moyer was nowhere to be found. Two witnesses were called who testified that they came to the coin shop that Saturday afternoon, knocked on the door and received no response. One of these witnesses actually returned an hour later and still had no success in contacting Alex Moyer. All parties were adamant that the lights in the shop were on and that Mr. Moyer's blue Cadillac was parked in the location depicted in the photograph.

At trial, Jim Oliver did not adamantly dispute that the time of death occurred at approximately 10:00 a.m. He gave only a token argument that it may have been later when it was clear David and Betsy Stone were traveling to Las Vegas. As things turned out, the David Stone case had to be retried based on this issue—Jim Oliver's failure to aggressively contest the time of death.

Thursday, March 25, 1982 Visalia Times-Delta — 1B

state/local

Prosecution seeks to link Moyer case, Fresno slaying

By MARY PITMAN
Times-Delta Staff Writer

The jade figurine had a handmade price tag on it. When Visalia Police Sgt. Bill Wittman scoured the vacated home of murder defendant David Stone, he found that price tag in a crawl-space beneath the home, according to Deputy District Attorney Ronn Couillard.

Out of the hearing of a Superior Court jury late Wednesday, Couillard argued that tag was one justification for introducing what is from the defense point of view highly prejudicial evidence, showing that Stone, on trial for the murder of a Visalia coinshop dealer, may also have been the last person to see Fresno coinshop dealer James Bibee alive.

Bibee, killed by 22-caliber bullet wounds, was found dead in the trunk of his car, some seven days after a rendezvous with Stone, Couillard said. That was two months before Alexander Frank Moyer Jr. was found dead in his U.S. Stamp and Coin shop on Murray Street.

Whether evidence attempting to link the two 1979 murders will be presented to the jury trying Stone for the Moyer murder is now up to Superior Court Judge Edward Kim. He postponed his ruling on the question Wednesday, to allow time for defense attorney James Oliver to submit written arguments against presentation of the evidence.

Couillard told Judge Kim that he could show that Stone made an appointment to buy a gold and silver coin collection from Bibee on Aug. 2, 1979. Bibee was supposed to meet Stone at Stone's house, Couillard said, and a friend of Bibee's, Harry Kelly, assisted Bibee in packaging the coin collection and the jade statue and placing them in the trunk of Bibee's car.

Kelly personally placed the price tag on the figurine, Couillard said. Thus when Sgt. Wittman later found a price tag in the Stone house, Kelly was able to identify the tag as the same one placed on the statue, the prosecutor said.

In a taped statement given to the Fresno police, Stone acknowledged the business transaction with Bibee but made no mention of the jade figurine, Couillard said.

No charges have been filed in the Fresno murder, court officials said outside the courtroom.

Those testifying Wednesday, the second day of Stone's trial, included Stone's father, Estym E. Stone Jr., a retired air traffic controller. The senior Stone testified that he did not think it was at all unusual when his son and wife dropped off their baby daughter for the grandparents to baby sit and then spent the night at a Fresno motel instead of at the defendant's Clovis home.

The prosecution is contending that Stone was trying to establish an alibi for himself, by checking into the Village Inn on the evening of Oct. 5, instead of staying at his own residence just a few miles away. Stone and his wife are known to have checked out at 10:58 a.m. on Saturday, Oct. 6. The prosecution contends that was about an hour after Moyer was shot while keeping an appointment with Stone in his shop.

But the elder Stone indicated that the motel was no alibi. "My son and his wife are pretty romantic and they had done this before at other hotels in town," he said.

Stone described his son, David, as being self-employed. David dealt in investments, old coins and silver and also penny stocks, Stone said. Those are low-priced stocks, less than a dollar in value, issued by companies just getting started in business, the defendant's father said.

In other testimony Wednesday, Fred Sciacca told the jury he sold a "junk silver" coin collection for $2,375 to murder victim Moyer on the Tuesday before his death. (The coins are valued for their silver contents.)

A friend of Moyer's, Harry E. Layman of Visalia, testified that he tried to negotiate the purchase of coins that same week for another friend, but Moyer told him the stocks he had on hand were all being held for a Fresno purchaser, wh[illegible] Sa[illegible]

Visalia Times-Delta, March 25, 1982.

Friday, March 26, 1982 Visalia Times-Delta — 1B

state/local

Judge permits attempt to link murders of two coin dealers

By MARY PITMAN
Times-Delta Staff Writer

Like the lens on a camera, the scope of a Superior Court murder trial widened Thursday to encompass testimony about a second murder — a second coin dealer's slaying in 1979.

Judge Edward Kim ruled Thursday that evidence may be admitted, attempting to link defendant David Stone with a gunshot slaying that happened two months prior to the one with which Stone, 24, is charged. He is charged with the Oct. 6, 1979, slaying of Visalia coinshop owner Alexander Frank Moyer Jr, 49.

The prosecution hopes to convince the jury that, on the Saturday he died, Moyer's last appointment — to sell a special stock of gold coins he told a friend he was reserving for a Fresno client — was with Stone.

Meanwhile, the prosecution also hopes to show that Stone was the last person to see Fresno coin dealer James Bibee alive. Bibee's body was found in August of 1979, in the trunk of a car abandoned in front of the Clovis police station. It was parked there six days after Bibee's last known appointment — with Stone.

Defense attorney James Oliver had argued against the admission of the Bibee evidence, contending that its prejudice to his client far outweighed any value it might have. Outside the courtroom, Oliver said the Bibee case was no more pertinent to the Visalia homicide than would be evidence concerning the slayings of two other coin dealers in the state, both killed since 1979 — one in Sacramento and the other in Bakersfield, Oliver said.

A taped conversation between the defendant and a Fresno police officer — played outside the hearing of the jury Thursday but which the jury was expected to hear today — reveals Stone's own version of what happened during his Aug. 2 appointment with Bibee.

In the Aug. 4 conversation, Stone told Officer Gary Snow that he had known Bibee for four years and that, as usual, Bibee came to Stone's house that afternoon.

Without any cash changing hands, Stone traded some Byzantine gold coins, worth about $700, to Bibee in exchange for 80 silver dollars, Stone said, in the tape.

"He (Bibee) didn't like to do that kind of business at the shop," Stone told the officer.

Not mentioned by Stone was a jade figurine that the prosecution hopes to show Bibee also traded to Stone. A key piece of evidence linking Stone to the Bibee case is the hand-lettered price tag, once on the figurine — a tag found by Sgt. Bill Wittman in searching the crawl-space underneath Stone's vacated home.

Stone said Bibee left his house about 6:30 p.m. that evening. As Stone watched Bibee drive away, Stone said he saw Bibee pause at the end of the block and pick up a dark-haired man who had just waved to him from the corner, Stone told Snow in the tape.

Stone recalled thinking that it wasn't smart to pick up hitch-hikers, but said, "at the time I didn't really

(See MOYER, page 4B)

Moyer murder - - -

(Continued from page 1B)

think anything of it." But later the incident came to mind, he said, when Bibee hadn't shown up at at home that night or at work the next day and Stone received a call from Bibee's worried partner.

"He (the partner) almost accused me of having something to do with (Bibee's) disappearance," Stone said, at one point in the tape.

Stone was visibly shaken Thursday, after the decision to admit the evidence and specifically by the testimony of Laura Wilson, 24, a friend of Stone's wife, Betsy.

Wilson testified that she was with the couple when they received a telephone call on Aug. 3, a day after Stone's appointment with Bibee. Betsy answered the call and said her husband was not in the house, although Wilson said Stone was, in fact, there at the time. She testified that both Stone and his wife seemed very upset by the call.

Visalia Times-Delta, March 26, 1982.

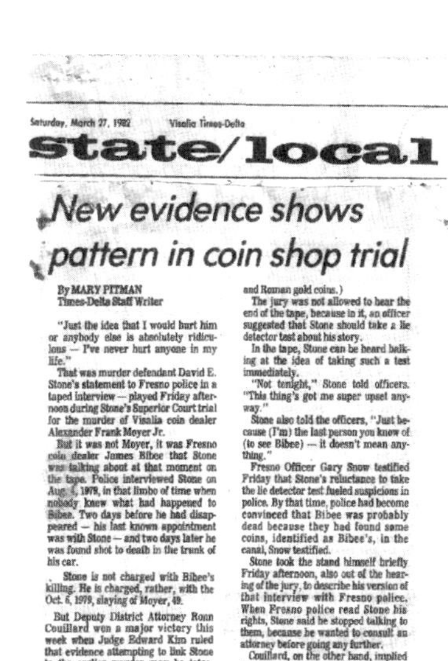

Saturday, March 27, 1982 Visalia Times-Delta

state/local

New evidence shows pattern in coin shop trial

By MARY PITMAN
Times-Delta Staff Writer

"Just the idea that I would hurt him or anybody else is absolutely ridiculous — I've never hurt anyone in my life."

That was murder defendant David E. Stone's statement to Fresno police in a taped interview — played Friday afternoon during Stone's Superior Court trial for the murder of Visalia coin dealer Alexander Frank Moyer Jr.

But it was not Moyer, it was Fresno coin dealer James Bibee that Stone was talking about at that moment on the tape. Police interviewed Stone on Aug. 4, 1979, in that limbo of time when nobody knew what had happened to Bibee. Two days before he had disappeared — his last known appointment was with Stone — and two days later he was found shot to death in the trunk of his car.

Stone is not charged with Bibee's killing. He is charged, rather, with the Oct. 6, 1979, slaying of Moyer, 49.

But Deputy District Attorney Ronn Couillard won a major victory this week when Judge Edward Kim ruled that evidence attempting to link Stone to the earlier murder may be introduced.

However, Stone's statement about not hurting anyone is included in the tail end of the tape — a portion that was played outside the hearing of the jury Friday afternoon. (Friday morning, the jury had already heard the rest of the interview, in which Stone describes what happened Aug. 2 when Bibee came to Stone's house to trade 80 silver dollars for some of Stone's Byzantine and Roman gold coins.)

The jury was not allowed to hear the end of the tape, because in it, an officer suggested that Stone should take a lie detector test about his story.

In the tape, Stone can be heard balking at the idea of taking such a test immediately.

"Not tonight," Stone told officers. "This thing's got me super upset anyway."

Stone also told the officers, "Just because (I'm) the last person you know of (to see Bibee) — it doesn't mean anything."

Fresno Officer Gary Snow testified Friday that Stone's reluctance to take the lie detector test fueled suspicions in police. By that time, police had become convinced that Bibee was probably dead because they had found some coins, identified as Bibee's, in the canal, Snow testified.

Stone took the stand himself briefly Friday afternoon, also out of the hearing of the jury, to describe his version of that interview with Fresno police. When Fresno police read Stone his rights, Stone said he stopped talking to them, because he wanted to consult an attorney before going any further.

Couillard, on the other hand, implied that Stone had told his wife he had gone fishing that day, when in fact he told officers he was walking, thinking some things over, in a Fresno shopping center.

But Stone denied those stories, during cross-examination from Couillard Friday.

With the jury back in the courtroom Friday, a Fresno pathologist testified that Bibee was killed by 10 bullet wounds to the chest area.

Visalia Times-Delta, March 27, 1982.

One item of evidence that had been developed since the preliminary hearing was the missing .22-caliber handgun registered to Eston Stone. Believing that this was extremely important, I wanted to exploit it as much as possible. Although it was true that the victims, Bibee and Moyer, were killed by separate .22-caliber firearms, neither of which was ever located, it seemed more than a coincidence that Eston Stone's .22 was reported as having been stolen the day before the Moyer murder.

When Eston Stone turned in the report of the stolen gun, the police dispatcher who took the report filled out a small card with the vital information concerning the theft. That information reflected that the gun was reported stolen at noon on Friday, October 5, 1979, from under the front seat of a car parked at the Straw Hat Pizza establishment in Clovis. The information indicated that the vehicle involved was the "complainant's car" (Eston Stone's car). Although Eston Stone had told Wittman and other officers at the time of executing the search warrant that the weapon was stolen from Betsy's car, we were aware that he was going to testify at trial that the gun was actually stolen from his daughter Holly's car. Thus at trial the jury would have three separate cars from which the gun was stolen—Betsy's, Holly's or Eston Stone's.

It was apparent that these conflicting stories concerning who was driving the car at the time of the alleged theft showed a degree of concern on the part of the defense. When something like this becomes apparent, the logical questions are: Why the concern? Is there a vulnerability there? By some backtracking and re-interviewing witnesses, Wittman discovered a small yet most significant occurrence that answered the question of who was driving the car and just why the defense was so concerned.

Laura Wilson was a high school friend of Betsy Stone whom I called as a witness. An attractive, blond-haired, blue-eyed girl in her early twenties, she had remained in contact with Betsy after her marriage to David Stone. On

June 12, 1979, the day after her twenty-first birthday, Laura had driven from her hometown of Le Grand to the Backer Street address in Fresno where the Stones were living at the time. Her plans were to spend three or four days visiting Betsy, as well as looking for a job in the Fresno area. On June 12, she accompanied Betsy and David to Visalia, where David sold a silver bar to Plunkett Coins. She remembered this because the coin shop was located in the center of town and she and Betsy window-shopped while David was making the transaction. They did not go to Moyer's shop, which was located several blocks from the center of town.

It was during this visit that Betsy showed her a .22-caliber handgun that belonged to David's father. The gun was kept under the front seat of the car they were driving—a silver Toyota sedan owned by and registered to David's father. This was the same vehicle description given by Maxine Guthrie as the one driven by David Stone during the month of August when the Bibee investigation was going on. This gave a clearer meaning to the statement by Eston Stone to the police dispatcher when reporting the alleged gun theft that the weapon was taken from the "complainant's car."

Laura Wilson visited Betsy Stone again on August 3, less than two months after the June visit and the day after the disappearance of James Bibee. The reason for the visit was to celebrate the birthday of the Stones' young daughter. Upon her arrival, she sensed that something was wrong. Soon after she arrived, the telephone rang and Betsy answered. The call was for David, but he refused to take it, telling Betsy to tell the caller that he was out.

Laura stated, "David was very nervous." He left the house and returned several times and appeared to be quite upset. Later that morning, she and Betsy went shopping to buy a birthday cake, and she noted that Betsy also seemed "nervous and uptight." When Laura inquired about what was bothering her, Betsy informed her that a man David sold some coins to had disappeared.

Laura's testimony to these events, although not central to the crimes involved, was nevertheless very effective. She was a totally unbiased witness who related events that reflected what could be characterized as guilty demeanor by David Stone the day after the disappearance of James Bibee and also could indicate that David had access to his father's missing .22-caliber handgun. More importantly, her testimony raised the suspicion of David's involvement in the alleged theft of the gun the day before the murder of Alex Moyer.

The defense tried to counter the gun theft inferences by calling David's sister, Holly Newton, to testify. She claimed that she had the gun in her possession because her father had given it to her to carry for protection, as she worked nights at a local department store and had to drive home after dark. She said she kept the gun under the front seat of her car. On Friday, October 5, she went to lunch with Betsy and a girlfriend. Holly drove her car, parked in the restaurant parking lot and thought she had locked the car. However, upon returning after lunch, found it to be unlocked. She was unclear just when she allegedly discovered the gun missing; however, she related it missing to this incident. While her testimony to this point seemed somewhat credible, her explanation about what occurred when the police executed the search warrant at her parents' home some two years later did not seem reasonable.

Regarding the serving of the warrant, Holly testified that she arrived at the residence just as the police were entering. Along with other family members present, she was directed to have a seat at the dining room table while the police conducted the search. Although she admitted she was aware that the object of the search was for handguns owned by her father, and though she overheard conversation between her father and the police about the missing gun, she did not volunteer the information about her having possession of that gun and the circumstances of its alleged theft. This seemed incredible since her brother was in jail facing a murder charge, and the obvious inference from all that was taking place was that the police suspected this missing gun was the murder weapon used in the Alex Moyer killing. Her failure to say something to the police at this time severely affected her credibility before the jury.

After Holly testified, the defense called two witnesses who did not appear to help its cause at all. Ron Tellesco identified himself as the person who arrived at the coin shop during the afternoon on the Saturday of the killing and knocked on the door—although the lights were on inside and Alex Moyer's car was in the lot, no one answered the door. He indicated that he was a regular customer familiar with Moyer's operation and that this was a very unusual occurrence.

Next, the defense called Scott Guthrie, the ten-year-old son of Maxine Guthrie, who lived near the Stones on Backer Street. Scott contradicted his mother's version of the events regarding David Stone leaving his house the evening of James Bibee's disappearance. He testified that he saw David Stone drive his own car and follow an older model car down the street. However, he was consistent with his mother in testifying that he saw David walk back to his home a short while later. Curiously, Scott said David was holding something in his hand that was covered by a cloth. The hand the object was in was the hand away from where Scott and his mother and siblings were. The manner described by young Scott Guthrie gave the impression that David was attempting to conceal from them whatever was in his hand.

I still felt that David Stone would testify. At about fifteen minutes to twelve o'clock, Jim Oliver asked if we could break for lunch. The request was granted, and after observing what appeared to be a rather serious discussion between Oliver and David Stone, I got the impression that he would not testify. I later learned from Oliver that David had intended to take the witness stand; however, he began to change his mind when the defense case started. As it turned out, Oliver used the lunch hour trying to convince David that he would be better off if he did take the witness stand. What Oliver most likely did not know was what really happened on the evening that James Bibee disappeared, something that did not come out until David slipped up in his testimony in the second trial.

When we returned to the courtroom after lunch, Judge Kim told Oliver that he could call his next witness, to which Oliver announced, "Your Honor, the defense rests." In my opinion, this always has a rather dramatic effect in any trial because all the while the prosecution is building up its case, the jury, at least subconsciously, must wonder how the defendant would explain this or that occurrence. Even though they have been told before trial that the defendant does not have to testify, nevertheless there is a certain impact when it becomes a reality.

It was now Tuesday afternoon, April 6, and after we went over a few preliminary matters outside the presence of the jury, we began final arguments. My argument took up most of what was left of the afternoon. We were all ordered back at 9:00 a.m. the next day to conclude the summations. Oliver's argument focused mainly on the lack of evidence to convince the jury of guilt beyond a reasonable doubt. However, he did something that was rather unusual. This became the topic of conversation for a while among those familiar with the case and even got mentioned in the newspaper story of the trial.

He argued for more than five long hours, with the noon break in between. After we returned from lunch, his focus became that because there were no signs of a forced entry or a scuffle, it was just as likely that one of Moyer's customers or acquaintances might have been the killer. There were several people in the audience watching the proceedings. Among them was David Dye, who had testified on behalf of the prosecution that he had done some work for Moyer in the past and often came to the shop. He also had seen, from a distance of about one block, the lights on in the shop and Moyer's

Cadillac parked in the lot at 6:00 p.m. that Saturday night. As Oliver got rolling on whether one of the victim's acquaintances could have done the killing, he paused and, in a manner reminiscent of Perry Mason, pointed at David Dye and said, "The killer could well have been David Dye!" This became quite the topic during the next break. David Dye asked me outside the courtroom if I was going to charge him, whereupon Bill Wittman took out his handcuffs and pretended to arrest him.

I concluded my final summation, and Judge Kim instructed the jury. The members of the jury began deliberations at about 3:30 p.m. and at 5:00 p.m. were released for the night and asked to return the next morning at nine o'clock.

Waiting for a jury to arrive at a decision is like a child waiting to open presents on a Christmas morning. It's not that the outcome will necessarily be one of joy—it is the anticipation and wonder. The attorneys and the parties involved have an excited rush within their bodies in anticipation, and each time there is any movement or noise indicating that the jury may have a question or a verdict increases this rush tenfold. It does not matter how many cases one has tried as an attorney—the anticipation is always there, most especially in a big case such as the Stone trial.

When the jury indicated that it had a question at 3:40 p.m. that Thursday afternoon, I returned to Judge Kim's court fearing the worst. It never fails

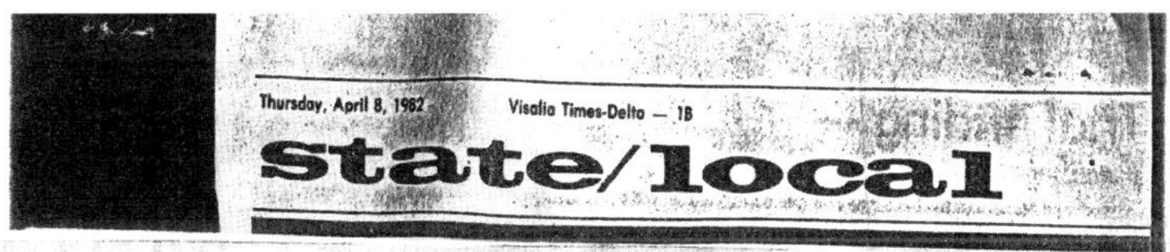

Thursday, April 8, 1982 Visalia Times-Delta — 1B

state/local

Coin shop murder trial ends in Perry Mason style

By MARY PITMAN
Times-Delta staff writer

He wasn't trying to stage a Perry Mason-style climax. Or so the defense attorney said.

But using that fictional attorney's dramatic tactics, Visalia attorney James Oliver attempted to briefly distract a Superior Court jury Wednesday from its focus on his client, David Stone. The jury began its deliberations late Wednesday.

Oliver alleged that another fair-haired young man named "David," seated at the rear of the courtroom, was just as likely to have murdered Visalia coin dealer Alexander Frank Moyer, Jr.

"Somebody played God with Mr. Moyer, but it wasn't my client," Oliver told the jury in his closing statement. "There are other people who are just as likely (to have done it)." The young man Oliver figuratively fingered was David Dye. Dye, a good friend of Moyer's, had worked part-time at the coin dealer's Murray Street shop, U.S. Stamp and Coin, for seven years, Dye testified.

Outside the courtroom, Dye did not seem perturbed by Oliver's insinuation. Indeed, he said, the theatrics in the courtroom had seemed somewhat comical to him. Dye said Oliver had told him, months before, that he might try to cast suspicions on him.

Deputy District Attorney Ronn Couillard, in his rebuttal argument Wednesday afternoon, indicated that Oliver's move was a feeble manuever. Dye was never a suspect in the case, Couillard said. He alleged that the insinuation was just one of many "red herrings" peppered throughout Oliver's defense.

Most of Oliver's closing statement Wednesday was spent in showing the jury that the web of circumstantial evidence woven by the prosecution had a number of gaping holes in it — all adding up to more than enough for a "reasonable doubt" to be left in the jury's mind, Oliver indicated.

One of the strange things about Moyer's Oct. 6, 1979, murder, police said at the time, was that the front door to the shop was locked when Moyer's body was glimpsed inside behind a counter. Firefighters had to be called to break in.

The killer would have had to lock the door with a key, from the outside, before he left. Dye had a key to the shop, Oliver pointed out Wednesday.

But Couillard said that it was more reasonable to assume Moyer's murderer locked the door when he left with a key that Moyer habitually kept inside the door-lock. The security-conscious coin dealer would turn the key in the lock to permit someone entry to the shop, and then turn the key again behind the visitor, testimony showed.

Oliver implied that someone who had his own key to the door must have done the slaying. He said Moyer's key was found in the door, as usual, when firefighters broke into the shop. In contrast, Couillard told the jury that Moyer's door key was missing. He said that the killer had obviously taken it with him and, outside, used it to lock the door.

Couillard's refrain throughout his prosecution closing statement Tuesday afternoon seemed to be, "It's more than a coincidence."

In ticking off what he termed the improbable coincidences surrounding Moyer's death, Couillard reminded the jury about a Bakersfield coin dealer's testimony in the case. Stone sold $9,000 worth of gold and silver to that dealer five days after Moyer's death, the dealer

(See TRIAL ENDING, page 2B)

Visalia Times-Delta, April 8, 1982.

when a jury has a question that the attorneys and even the judge will speculate on why that particular question and what it means in regard to where it is in arriving at a verdict. The jury in this case wanted the judge to reread the jury instruction defining reasonable doubt. I took this as a positive sign; it was my thought that maybe one or two jurors may have been undecided and that this definition—which reads in part that "all things relating to human affairs may be open to some possible or imaginary doubt"—was an effort on the part of the majority to pull these holdouts into their camp. This was apparently true, for within minutes after returning to the jury room, it announced that it had a verdict.

It took several minutes to round up all the parties. The father and stepmother of Alex Moyer, David Dye, Henry Lawson, Bill Wittman, Bill McGowen and several persons I did not recognize were in the courtroom, as were all of David Stone's family, including the now reappeared Betsy Stone and several of the office personnel from the District Attorney's Office. The usual formality occurred—Judge Kim had the foreman identify himself, asked if the group had arrived at a verdict and, upon being told it had, asked the foreman to hand the verdict form to the bailiff. The bailiff carried the verdict form to the bench and handed it to the judge, who looked it over to make sure it was properly signed and dated. Then the judge handed it to the court clerk to be read aloud.

"In the Superior Court of the State of California, in and for the County of Tulare, the People of the State of California, Plaintiff, David Edward Stone, Defendant, verdict, 20607, Visalia, California, April 8, 1982. We the jury find Defendant guilty of the offense of murder in violation of Penal

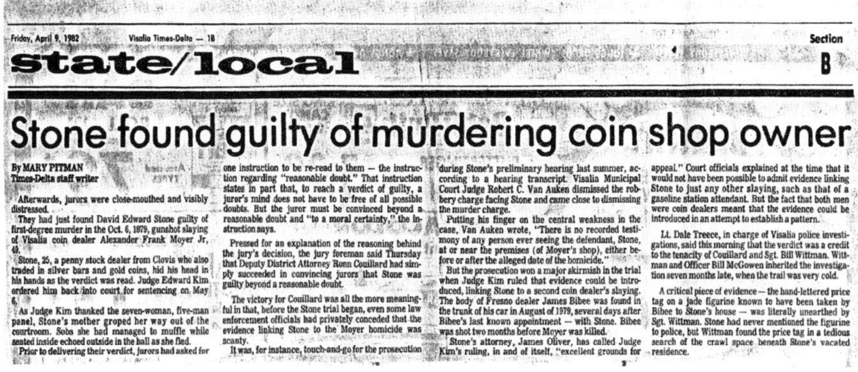

Friday, April 9, 1982 Visalia Times-Delta — 1B

state/local

Section B

Stone found guilty of murdering coin shop owner

By MARY PITMAN
Times-Delta staff writer

Afterwards, jurors were close-mouthed and visibly distressed.

They had just found David Edward Stone guilty of first-degree murder in the Oct. 6, 1979, gunshot slaying of Visalia coin dealer Alexander Frank Moyer Jr, 49.

Stone, 25, a penny stock dealer from Clovis who also traded in silver bars and gold coins, hid his head in his hands as the verdict was read. Judge Edward Kim ordered him back into court for sentencing on May 6.

As Judge Kim thanked the seven-woman, five-man panel, Stone's mother groped her way out of the courtroom. Sobs she had managed to muffle while seated inside echoed outside in the hall as she fled.

Prior to delivering their verdict, jurors had asked for one instruction to be re-read to them — the instruction regarding "reasonable doubt." That instruction states in part that, to reach a verdict of guilty, a juror's mind does not have to be free of all possible doubts. But the juror must be convinced beyond a reasonable doubt and "to a moral certainty," the instruction says.

Pressed for an explanation of the reasoning behind the jury's decision, the jury foreman said Thursday that Deputy District Attorney Ronn Couillard had simply succeeded in convincing jurors that Stone was guilty beyond a reasonable doubt.

The victory for Couillard was all the more meaningful in that, before the Stone trial began, even some law enforcement officials had privately conceded that the evidence linking Stone to the Moyer homicide was scanty.

It was, for instance, touch-and-go for the prosecution during Stone's preliminary hearing last summer, according to a hearing transcript. Visalia Municipal Court Judge Robert C. Van Auken dismissed the robbery charge facing Stone and came close to dismissing the murder charge.

Putting his finger on the central weakness in the case, Van Auken wrote, "There is no recorded testimony of any person ever seeing the defendant, Stone, at or near the premises (of Moyer's shop), either before or after the alleged date of the homicide."

But the prosecution won a major skirmish in the trial when Judge Kim ruled that evidence could be introduced, linking Stone to a second coin dealer's slaying. The body of Fresno dealer James Bibee was found in the trunk of his car in August of 1979, several days after Bibee's last known appointment — with Stone. Bibee was shot two months before Moyer was killed.

Stone's attorney, James Oliver, has called Judge Kim's ruling, in and of itself, "excellent grounds for appeal." Court officials explained at the time that it would not have been possible to admit evidence linking Stone to just any other slaying, such as that of a gasoline station attendant. But the fact that both men were coin dealers meant that the evidence could be introduced in an attempt to establish a pattern.

Lt. Dale Treece, in charge of Visalia police investigations, said this morning that the verdict was a credit to the tenacity of Couillard and Sgt. Bill Wittman. Wittman and Officer Bill McGowen inherited the investigation seven months late, when the trail was very cold.

A critical piece of evidence — the hand-lettered price tag on a jade figurine known to have been taken by Bibee to Stone's house — was literally unearthed by Sgt. Wittman. Stone had never mentioned the figurine to police, but Wittman found the price tag in a tedious search of the crawl space beneath Stone's vacated residence.

Visalia Times-Delta, April 9, 1982.

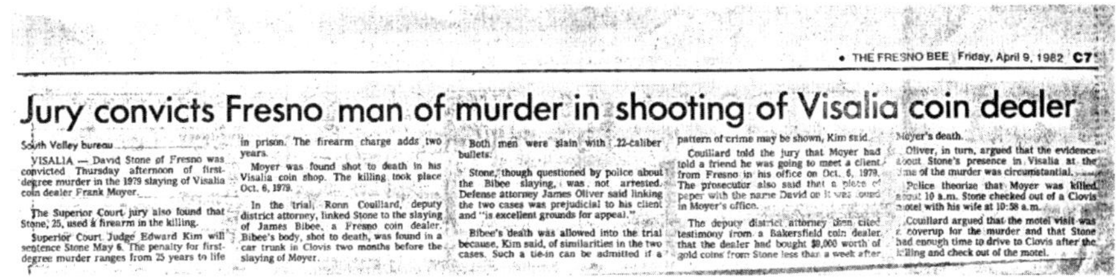

• THE FRESNO BEE Friday, April 9, 1982 C7

Jury convicts Fresno man of murder in shooting of Visalia coin dealer

South Valley bureau

VISALIA — David Stone of Fresno was convicted Thursday afternoon of first-degree murder in the 1979 slaying of Visalia coin dealer Frank Moyer.

The Superior Court jury also found that Stone, 25, used a firearm in the killing.

Superior Court Judge Edward Kim will sentence Stone May 6. The penalty for first-degree murder ranges from 25 years to life in prison. The firearm charge adds two years.

Moyer was found shot to death in his Visalia coin shop. The killing took place Oct. 6, 1979.

In the trial, Ronn Couillard, deputy district attorney, linked Stone to the slaying of James Bibee, a Fresno coin dealer. Bibee's body, shot to death, was found in a car trunk in Clovis two months before the slaying of Moyer.

Both men were slain with .22-caliber bullets.

Stone, though questioned by police about the Bibee slaying, was not arrested. Defense attorney James Oliver said linking the two cases was prejudicial to his client and "is excellent grounds for appeal."

Bibee's death was allowed into the trial because, Kim said, of similarities in the two cases. Such a tie-in can be admitted if a pattern of crime may be shown, Kim said.

Couillard told the jury that Moyer had told a friend he was going to meet a client from Fresno in his office on Oct. 6, 1979. The prosecutor also said that a piece of paper with the name David on it was found in Moyer's office.

The deputy district attorney then cited testimony from a Bakersfield coin dealer that the dealer had bought $9,000 worth of gold coins from Stone less than a week after Moyer's death.

Oliver, in turn, argued that the evidence about Stone's presence in Visalia at the time of the murder was circumstantial.

Police theorize that Moyer was killed about 10 a.m. Stone checked out of a Clovis motel with his wife at 10:58 a.m.

Couillard argued that the motel visit was a coverup for the murder and that Stone had enough time to drive to Clovis after the killing and check out of the motel.

Fresno Bee, April 9, 1982.

Code 187 as charged in the Information and find said murder to be in the first degree." The jury also found true the allegation that he personally used a firearm in the commission of the murder. I turned to Wittman, who was seated next to me at the counsel table. He sat there with a big smile on his face and whispered, "We got him" as the judge thanked and excused the jury. I stole a glance at David Stone; his face was blushed red, and he was shaking his head back and forth as though in disbelief.

That evening, Charlotte and I went out to dinner with the Moyers and the Wittmans. It was a most pleasant time. Little did we know that we would have to do this all over again in two years.

THE APPEAL

David Stone's attorney filed a motion for a new trial, which is normal procedure following a conviction. The motion was denied by Judge Kim, and Stone was sentenced to state prison for twenty-seven years to life on May 6, 1981. We all knew that the usual appeal would follow. My only concern was that the appellate court might decide that the use of the Bibee murder evidence as an uncharged prior criminal act was improper. I was certain in my mind that it was properly admitted; however, as a prosecutor, especially in the 1970s and '80s in California, one could never be sure the liberal appellate court judges would not decide otherwise. There appeared to be no other issue in the trial that could give rise to even the remotest chance of a reversal.

The California Fifth District Court of Appeal, located in Fresno, is the appellate court that hears appeals from Tulare County. It had a reputation in those days of being a very liberal court, having overturned many criminal convictions on the most technical of issues. On February 22, 1984, the Fifth

District did it again in the David Stone case. The verdict was not overturned on the Bibee evidence, but rather on something much more frustrating. In its opinion, the three-judge appellate court upheld the trial court's ruling allowing the Bibee evidence by a vote of two to one. However, the opinion stated that when the case is retried, this issue must be addressed anew, and the next trial court would be free to reject such evidence if it felt warranted. A reading of the opinion gave one the distinct impression that the court felt the jury should not have found David Stone guilty and it was going to set that verdict aside.

The case was overturned and remanded for retrial because of "newly discovered evidence" and "ineffective assistance of counsel." The essence of the reversal was that Jim Oliver failed to adequately investigate, and/or present and argue, certain evidence that the appellate attorney labeled newly discovered. This involved a rather technical procedural situation. Stone's appellate attorney had appealed the conviction on several issues, one of which was the Bibee evidence, and the court ruled that there was no trial error that could give rise to a reversal and remand for retrial. At the same time, the appellate attorney filed a writ of habeas corpus alleging that Stone was held in custody illegally since newly discovered evidence had been found that created a reasonable belief that he was not guilty. This newly discovered evidence consisted of a rehashing of the facts of the case. It centered on three factual issues.

The main focus was the "coffee pot evidence." This consisted of the fact that in his report Bill McGowen had written that upon entering the coin shop they "found a Mr. Coffee coffee-maker still warming a small amount of coffee." Based on this, the defense had a test run through a laboratory in Oakland, California, to determine the evaporation rate of coffee under similar circumstances. Using a Mr. Coffee coffee maker and the same type of coffee as found in Moyer's shop and using relatively the same temperature as would have been present in Moyer's shop that October weekend, the test concluded that to have the amount of coffee purportedly remaining in the coffeepot when the police arrived at the murder scene, the coffee would have had to start brewing sometime late Saturday afternoon or evening, a time when Stone was conceded to have been on his way to Las Vegas.

There were many problems with this scenario. First, McGowen, who admitted that he is not a coffee drinker and thus was totally unfamiliar with coffee makers, could not remember distinctly whether the coffee maker was turned off or on. The photographs of the scene were not totally conclusive on this issue. (Note, all photographs of the coffeepot were inadvertently destroyed following the second trial.) Some appear to show the red light, which indicates the brewing or warming phase, to be on, while other photos definitely show the light to be off. This raises a crucial question. Was the light always off, and do those photos that would appear to show it on do so because of the lighting condition and/or glare inside the coin shop? The defense testing proceeded on two assumptions. First, that the heating element on Moyer's coffee maker was working properly, and two, that the coffee maker was in the "on" position when the police arrived.

However, in a test done later through the State of California Department of Justice Criminal Laboratory, it was determined that the coffee maker was in an "off" position. This fact was verified by the Department of Justice laboratory in that it actually re-created the police photographs in its testing procedure. Again, assuming that the heating element was working properly, the laboratory ran two separate tests and took photographs of the results, one photograph with the coffee maker left in the "on" position and another with it turned "off." In each test, it reduced the contents of the coffeepot to the level that was shown in the police photographs. These tests were designed to cover either scenario (i.e., whether the coffee maker was on or off when the police arrived on the crime scene).

Photographs taken while in the "on" position showed condensation on the sides of the coffeepot above the liquid level. Photographs taken in the "off" position clearly showed no condensation on the sides of the coffeepot above the remaining liquid. The police photographs taken at the time clearly showed *no* condensation on the sides of the coffeepot. Thus the conclusion that the coffee maker was not "on" that Sunday morning when the police photographs were taken.

Other questions that could not be answered and thus might reflect on the accuracy of any test included how much liquid was actually left in the pot (the photos were not totally clear); what if Moyer reheated some old coffee as opposed to brewing a new pot and, if so, what effect would this have; and what was the actual room temperature in the coin shop during this time span and what effect, if any, would it have. Since none of these questions could be answered, it would be mere speculation to factor these into the results.

The second area wherein the appellate court chose to second-guess the representation by Jim Oliver had to do with the mail delivered by Joe Diaz that Saturday morning. Diaz testified that the usual Saturday morning procedure was for him to knock on the door, Moyer to greet him and converse briefly and Diaz to hand him the mail. Because Moyer did not answer the door on this occasion, Diaz testified in passing that he dropped the mail through the mail slot in the door. The appellate court then made a factual finding. It bought the appellate attorney's argument that because the police photographs of the inside of the coin shop did not show any mail on the floor where it presumably would have dropped, it was, ipso facto, true that Moyer must have picked up the mail delivered by Joe Diaz at approximately 10:45 a.m. Thus he was alive at this hour, a few minutes before Stone was about to check out of the motel in Fresno. Therefore, the logical conclusion was that he could not have killed Moyer at close to 10:00 a.m. to fit within the prosecution's timeline.

A thorough analysis of all the police photographs make clear that there is *not* a mail slot in the door of the coin shop. This door is total glass with a metal frame around it and two metal bars across it in the middle. One of these metal bars across the middle is on the inside and one on the outside of the door. A handle is attached to each of these metal bars. The photos also clearly show two metal mailboxes attached to the outside wall of the coin shop. These two mailboxes are located in a narrow space between the door to Moyer's shop and the door to the adjoining business. These mailboxes were located one slightly above the other. The underneath one was clearly marked "1134," and the one above it did not have an address on it; however, immediately above the glass door to the coin shop is the address "1136." Thus it was obvious that any mail for either the coin shop or the adjoining business would normally be left in these metal mailboxes. (Note, at some time afterward, these two shops' addresses were changed; the coin shop was designated as "1134" and the adjoining shop as "1132.") Simply stated: Diaz was mistaken. He had placed the mail in Moyer's metal mailbox when he could get no response from inside the coin shop. The photographs were admitted as evidence and were part of the record, thus they were available to clarify this issue.

The last area where the court found some facts justifying a new trial had to do with testimony of several witnesses, primarily the Heslingas. Dale Heslinga had testified that he looked through the glass door of the coin shop Saturday evening and did not see Moyer. In addition, several other witnesses indicated that they came to the coin shop that Saturday morning, looked through the glass door and did not see anyone inside. Then, the next morning, Dale Heslinga was able to see a small portion of Moyer's body on the floor behind the counter when he looked through a small open space in the *window*—not the glass door. The witness testimony, along with the photographs of the building, clearly show that the small open space in

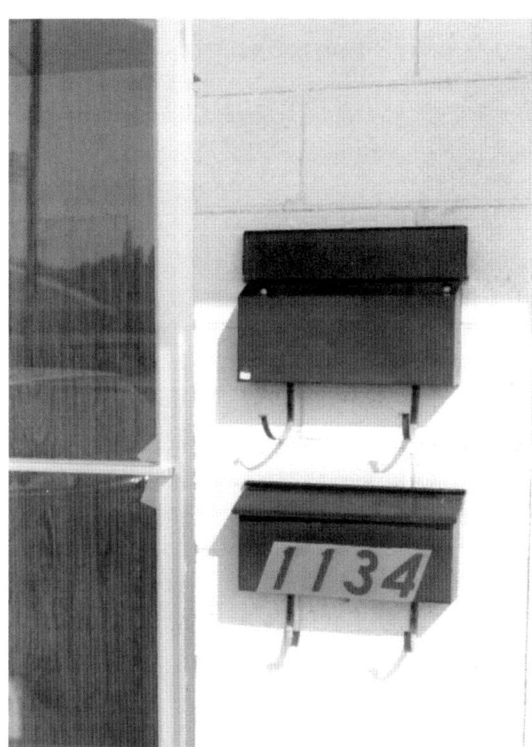

Right: Mailboxes for the coin shop (*top*) and the adjoining office. *Courtesy of Visalia Police Department.*

Below: Glass door to coin shop with address above the door. *Courtesy of Visalia Police Department.*

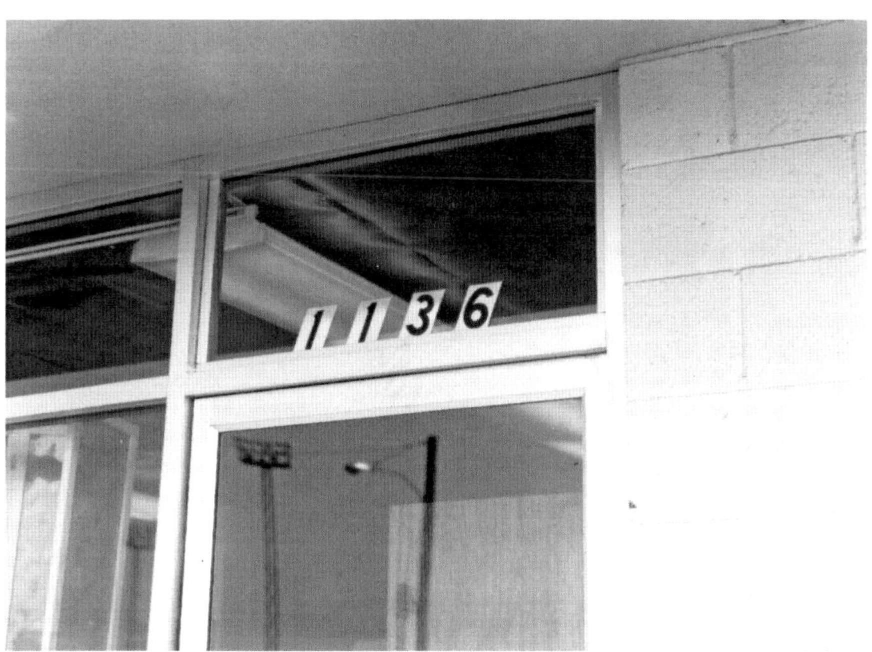

the window was several feet from the glass door. Thus it gave a different view of the inside of the coin shop.

Based on this bare testimony, the court came to the conclusion that Moyer must not have been lying dead on the floor behind the counter on Saturday evening, that he must have been killed later Saturday night after the Heslingas came to the shop. This assertion has no basis in logic because when they returned Sunday morning and looked through the glass door, they still could not see the victim. However, a clear reading of the trial transcript would reveal that both Dale and Barbara Heslinga testified that they needed to look through the small open space in the window—a vantage point different than the one they used on Saturday—to see Moyer's arm sticking out from behind the counter. Their Saturday vantage point was through the glass door, the same door through which all other persons who came to the shop that Saturday also looked.

Because it became evident to all throughout the trial that Alex Moyer was nowhere to be found when all evidence pointed to the fact that he should have been in the shop, these issues never came into controversy and were tacitly conceded by the defense. To dispute them would have run the risk of losing credibility with the jury. Nevertheless, the appellate court chose to second-guess Jim Oliver.

The court identified the term "new evidence" as any evidence not presented at the trial. It further noted that the standard of proof in the habeas corpus proceeding is "by a preponderance of the evidence."

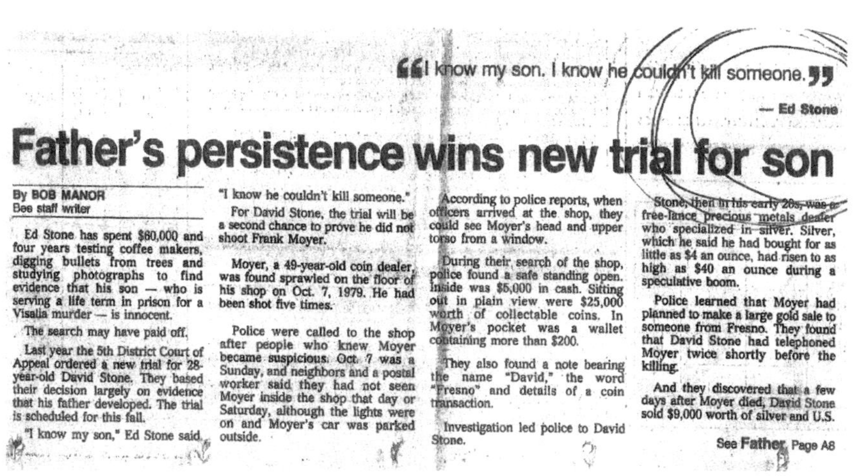

"I know my son. I know he couldn't kill someone."

— Ed Stone

Father's persistence wins new trial for son

By BOB MANOR
Bee staff writer

Ed Stone has spent $60,000 and four years testing coffee makers, digging bullets from trees and studying photographs to find evidence that his son — who is serving a life term in prison for a Visalia murder — is innocent.

The search may have paid off.

Last year the 5th District Court of Appeal ordered a new trial for 28-year-old David Stone. They based their decision largely on evidence that his father developed. The trial is scheduled for this fall.

"I know my son," Ed Stone said. "I know he couldn't kill someone."

For David Stone, the trial will be a second chance to prove he did not shoot Frank Moyer.

Moyer, a 49-year-old coin dealer, was found sprawled on the floor of his shop on Oct. 7, 1979. He had been shot five times.

Police were called to the shop after people who knew Moyer became suspicious. Oct. 7 was a Sunday, and neighbors and a postal worker said they had not seen Moyer inside the shop that day or Saturday, although the lights were on and Moyer's car was parked outside.

According to police reports, when officers arrived at the shop, they could see Moyer's head and upper torso from a window.

During their search of the shop, police found a safe standing open. Inside was $5,000 in cash. Sitting out in plain view were $25,000 worth of collectable coins. In Moyer's pocket was a wallet containing more than $200.

They also found a note bearing the name "David," the word "Fresno" and details of a coin transaction.

Investigation led police to David Stone.

Stone, then in his early 20s, was a free-lance precious metals dealer who specialized in silver. Silver, which he said he had bought for as little as $4 an ounce, had risen to as high as $40 an ounce during a speculative boom.

Police learned that Moyer had planned to make a large gold sale to someone from Fresno. They found that David Stone had telephoned Moyer twice shortly before the killing.

And they discovered that a few days after Moyer died, David Stone sold $9,000 worth of silver and U.S.

See Father, Page A8

David Stone wins appeal to get new trial. *From the* Fresno Bee.

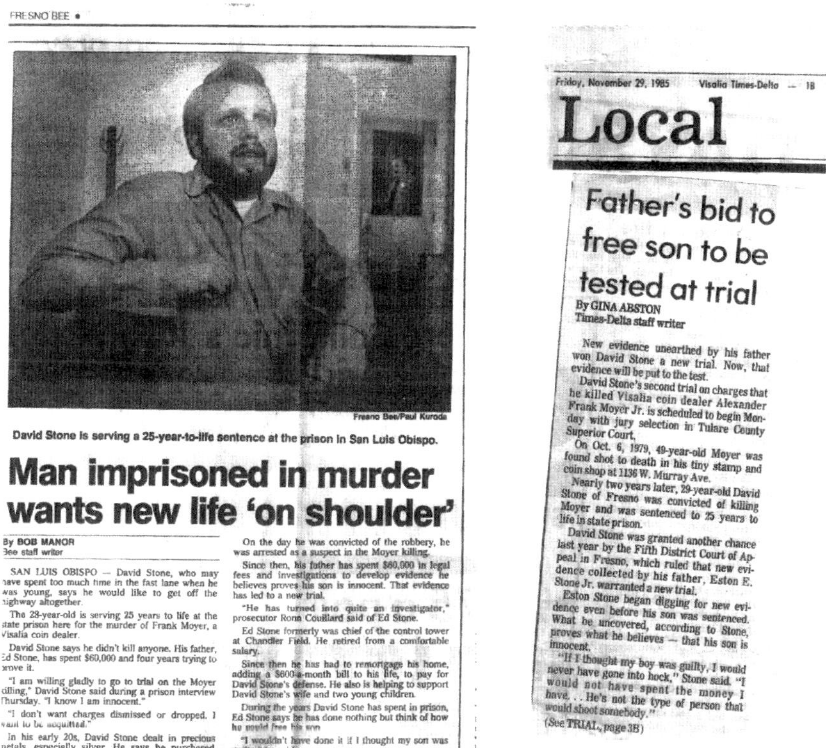

FRESNO BEE •

Fresno Bee/Paul Kuroda

David Stone is serving a 25-year-to-life sentence at the prison in San Luis Obispo.

Man imprisoned in murder wants new life 'on shoulder'

By BOB MANOR
Bee staff writer

SAN LUIS OBISPO — David Stone, who may have spent too much time in the fast lane when he was young, says he would like to get off the highway altogether.

The 28-year-old is serving 25 years to life at the state prison here for the murder of Frank Moyer, a Visalia coin dealer.

David Stone says he didn't kill anyone. His father, Ed Stone, has spent $60,000 and four years trying to prove it.

"I am willing gladly to go to trial on the Moyer killing," David Stone said during a prison interview Thursday. "I know I am innocent."

"I don't want charges dismissed or dropped. I want to be acquitted."

In his early 20s, David Stone dealt in precious metals, especially silver. He says he purchased

On the day he was convicted of the robbery, he was arrested as a suspect in the Moyer killing.

Since then, his father has spent $60,000 in legal fees and investigations to develop evidence he believes proves his son is innocent. That evidence has led to a new trial.

"He has turned into quite an investigator," prosecutor Ronn Couillard said of Ed Stone.

Ed Stone formerly was chief of the control tower at Chandler Field. He retired from a comfortable salary.

Since then he has had to remortgage his home, adding a $600-a-month bill to his life, to pay for David Stone's defense. He also is helping to support David Stone's wife and two young children.

During the years David Stone has spent in prison, Ed Stone says he has done nothing but think of how he would free his son.

"I wouldn't have done it if I thought my son was

Friday, November 29, 1985 Visalia Times-Delta — 1B

Local

Father's bid to free son to be tested at trial

By GINA ABSTON
Times-Delta staff writer

New evidence unearthed by his father won David Stone a new trial. Now, that evidence will be put to the test.

David Stone's second trial on charges that he killed Visalia coin dealer Alexander Frank Moyer Jr. is scheduled to begin Monday with jury selection in Tulare County Superior Court.

On Oct. 6, 1979, 49-year-old Moyer was found shot to death in his tiny stamp and coin shop at 1136 W. Murray Ave.

Nearly two years later, 29-year-old David Stone of Fresno was convicted of killing Moyer and was sentenced to 25 years to life in state prison.

David Stone was granted another chance last year by the Fifth District Court of Appeal in Fresno, which ruled that new evidence collected by his father, Eston E. Stone Jr. warranted a new trial.

Eston Stone began digging for new evidence even before his son was sentenced. What he uncovered, according to Stone, proves what he believes — that his son is innocent.

"If I thought my boy was guilty, I would never have gone into hock," Stone said. "I would not have spent the money I have. . . He's not the type of person that would shoot somebody."

(See TRIAL, page 3B)

Left: David Stone interview after winning appeal. *From the* Fresno Bee.

Right: *Visalia Times-Delta*, November 29, 1985.

Because the defense did not raise these areas of exculpatory evidence at trial, the verdict was overturned and a new trial ordered. Such is the power of the appellate court. So, whether we agreed or not, David Stone would get a new trial.

The second trial was basically a rehash of the first trial with two rather significant twists. Jim Oliver did not represent Stone this second time around. Because the Stone family had exhausted their funds on the first trial and the appeal, David told the court that he could not raise the money to hire his own counsel, whereupon the trial court appointed an attorney to represent him. The U.S. Supreme Court had ruled in a famous 1963 case that those charged with a criminal offense have the right to be represented by counsel, and if they were indigent, the court had to appoint counsel to represent them at court expense.

A local attorney named Tom Simonian was appointed to defend David Stone in the second trial. Tom had been an attorney for more than ten years at this time and was in private practice with another attorney in Visalia. Having spent several years in the Tulare County Public Defender's Office, he was an experienced criminal trial attorney and had defended several persons charged with murder. Like Jim Oliver, he was a congenial and pleasant person to work with, unlike some defense attorneys who think that every conversation and court appearance is either out-and-out warfare or some cunning con game wherein they must compete in "one up-man-ship."

David Stone was transported from the state prison to Tulare County to stand trial, and a trial date was eventually set for December 3, 1985, in Judge Jay Ballantyne's court.

The Pillsbury Doughboy had changed somewhat during his stay in the California state prison system. He still looked the part of the famous talking biscuit; however, he had "toughened up" in his attitude and mannerisms. He had a slight swagger in his walk, and his speech had a slightly detectable rough edge that can be associated with a "tough guy" image, both of which were definitely not present at the time of his first trial.

We had another hearing in front of Judge Ballantyne on the admissibility of the Bibee murder evidence, and it was ruled admissible. This ruling, although I fully expected it since the appellate court had indicated that such evidence was properly admissible, nevertheless was a major part of my case and was a major factor in proving Stone's guilt. There was also an added bonus involved in the Bibee evidence in the second trial that came as a complete shock to me and, I am sure, to Tom Simonian as well. That bonus came in the form of David Stone testifying in the trial.

Taking the witness stand and testifying in an attempt to clear himself of any wrongdoing, he denied having anything to do with the murder of James Bibee. However, he admitted to lying to the police during the Bibee investigation, and just as significantly, he admitted to inducing his wife to also lie to the police. This latter admission verified all of our suspicions as to why Betsy had not shown up to testify in the first trial. She was afraid of committing perjury on the witness stand.

These admissions came about rather innocently during his direct testimony in explaining the events surrounding the Bibee murder. David said something that inferred that Betsy and their young daughter had gone to visit her parents' home in Le Grand that Thursday, August 2, 1979. At that point, Simonian did not pursue any more questioning about the Bibee incident and turned his attention to the events of Saturday, October 6, the day the Stones left for Las Vegas. David appeared quite confident discussing those events. He described in detail the journey from Fresno south to Bakersfield, stopping for lunch and then traveling to Las Vegas and arriving just before 6:00 p.m. He even went into detail how he called his father twice while en route as they had agreed he would. This was because he was having some car trouble, and they wanted to be sure that they arrived at their destination before the father left his home that day. Curiously, David confirmed the statement that Betsy had given to the police that upon awakening that Saturday morning at the motel, David was gone. He returned just before they checked out at 10:58 a.m. and told her he had gone to have the car checked in preparation for their trip. Thus the window of opportunity was there for him to drive to Visalia, kill and rob Alex Moyer and return to the motel in time to check out at 10:58 a.m. Despite this rather obvious area of vulnerability in respect to the Moyer killing, David testified confidently to all of these events.

It was in testifying about the Bibee killing that one could detect an obvious and apparent nervousness, annoyance and shiftiness on his part. Sensing this, I tended to probe about in respect to the Bibee visit to his home that day when suddenly he slipped up and admitted that Betsy was not present when Mr. Bibee came to the Backer Street house. Rarely, if ever, does an attorney during trial have the experience of a witness admitting on cross-examination that they lied to the police regarding a material fact and, further, admitting that he forced another person to also lie to the police. This is what happened as David Stone was cross-examined.

Still maintaining his innocence of any wrongdoing involved in the Bibee murder, he nevertheless admitted that he felt pressured because he was supposedly the last person to see Mr. Bibee. Knowing that they would most likely accuse him of some involvement in James Bibee's disappearance, he induced his wife to tell the Fresno police that she was home during the time Bibee visited their home when, in fact, she had taken their daughter to visit her parents and did not return to Fresno until late that evening. Watching David Stone squirm, shift, stutter, blink and turn red during this portion of his testimony was well worth the price of admission. His guilt of the murder of James Bibee was showing through ever so clearly as he struggled to justify these actions.

The pieces of the Bibee puzzle, which we always knew were there, were verified by this admission. The reason David was seen by his neighbors, Maxine Guthrie and her son, walking back to the house carrying something wrapped in a red cloth was because he had ridden off with Bibee in Bibee's car. He then directed him to some remote location (the Backer Street home was at the edge of a large, sparsely populated area in the foothills east of Fresno and Clovis), shot him, placed the body in the trunk and walked back to his home. He did not have access to his car until Betsy returned home later that evening. Even Betsy told the police that David left the house several times after she arrived home and before the arrival of her friend Laura Wilson the next day. These would have been trips to the location of Bibee's vehicle to check on the body and remove whatever belongings of Bibee he wanted to keep or throw around various residential streets to confuse the police. Typical of David, however, because he could not stand the pressure of the police being unable to locate Bibee, he "helped" them by driving Bibee's old Chevrolet, complete with body in the trunk, to the Clovis Police Station.

Although I was convinced of his guilt of the Moyer murder, I could not believe that the Fresno district attorney refused to file against him for the Bibee murder. I even told Detectives Snow and Reynolds in jest, although I actually was serious, to tell the Fresno D.A.'s office that if none of its attorneys was willing to try the Bibee case, I would take a vacation from my present duties and prosecute the matter without pay. The irony of the whole situation was that if the Bibee murder were prosecuted in Fresno, the Moyer murder in Visalia would come in as circumstantial evidence of identity, just as the Bibee evidence was used in the Moyer trial.

The other surprise in the second trial was that the much ballyhooed "coffee pot evidence" was never offered by the defense. This came about in a rather unusual manner. Because I had the report from the Department of Justice lab in Fresno that determined that the coffeepot was most likely not even turned on at the time of the Moyer killing, I was waiting to confront the defense analyst with this determination and the evidence supporting it and hopefully eliminate any credibility to the so-called defense. Before the trial, I had given the defense a copy of this report pursuant to the California Rules of Discovery in criminal cases.

The defense had started its presentation of evidence in the morning by calling Eston Stone and a few other miscellaneous witnesses. Tom Simonian had planned on calling Chester Miller, the analyst who had conducted the coffeepot analysis for the defense, as the first witness after the lunch break since he was driving a long distance and would not arrive until late morning. We had taken a short recess in midmorning when a court clerk told Tom he had a call from his office.

Tom left, and upon his return, he was noticeably upset. Requesting to consult with both me and Judge Ballantyne in the judge's chambers, he informed us that he was most likely not going to present the coffeepot evidence. He said that he had just then received word from his analyst that there had been some "erroneous calculations" made. Rather than being able to conclude that the latest the coffee could have been brewed would have been sometime around 6:00 p.m. that Saturday, it now appeared that it could have been brewed "around noon" on Saturday. Presumably, Chester Miller had gone over his calculations in preparation for his testimony and discovered the error that morning. My belief was that he had reviewed the Fresno lab's conclusions that the coffee maker was most likely in an "off" position, could not in good faith refute that conclusion and, rather than agree with it, told the defense attorney that his calculations were in error, thus implying that although he still maintained the coffee maker was "on," it would not necessarily benefit the defense claim. Simonian said that he had to think the matter over during the lunch break and decide whether he would offer this evidence.

When we returned from the lunch break, Tom told us he was making a tactical decision not to present the "coffee pot evidence." To protect himself from being criticized later for not presenting such potentially crucial evidence, he placed on the record the reason for his decision. He indicated that in his studied opinion, the analysis had lost much of its credibility, as had the analyst due to his last-minute flip-flop in the conclusion. The potential of an obvious discrediting of Mr. Miller during cross-examination would only further diminish the defense credibility. Plus there was the fact that this evidence, countered by the Fresno lab's apparently credible analysis, would

Tuesday, December 17, 1985 Visalia Times-Delta — 3A

Stone found guilty for the second time

By GINA ABSTON
Times-Delta staff writer

Betsy Stone's sobs filled the courtroom Monday as the verdict was read. For the second time, her husband was found guilty of first-degree murder.

After deliberating for nearly a day, jurors in Tulare County Superior Court found David Stone, 29, guilty in the 1979 shooting death of Visalia coin dealer Alexander Frank Moyer.

Moyer, 49, was found dead in his small stamp and coin shop at 1136 W. Murray Ave. Police believe Stone stole expensive gold coins from the shop after killing Moyer, however theft charges were not pressed because the prosecution lacked evidence.

Stone seemed annoyed with the verdict. As his wife's cries grew louder, he turned around and told her, "I expected it." When Judge Jay R. Ballantyne asked the Fresno man if he waived his right to be sentenced by Jan. 13, Stone replied "What rights? Yeah, I do. . . I'll be here."

Stone's sentencing was scheduled for Jan. 14. He is expected to be handed 27 years to life in state prison — the same sentence he received in 1980 when he was first convicted of murder.

That 1980 conviction was overturned about a year ago by the Fifth District Court of Appeal, which granted Stone a second trial after reviewing new evidence uncovered by his father.

Outside the courtroom, Stone's father, Eston, declined to comment on the verdict. Standing beside him, with her forehead pressed against a chilled window, Betsy Stone continued to weep.

Stone is serving his murder sentence at the California Men's Colony in San Luis Obispo, where he is also serving a five-year sentence for robbing diamonds from a Clovis jewelry store.

After hearing Monday's verdict, defense attorney Thomas Simonian said evidence linking Stone to the uncharged murder of Fresno coin dealer James Bibbee two months before Moyer's killing was "too overwhelming" for jurors.

"I feel very strongly that it was an incorrect ruling, and I'm sure it will be dealt with on appeal," Simonian said.

The decision to allow the Bibbee case to be introduced to jurors was made in Superior Court and upheld in appellate court. Simonian said he expects the issue to go as far as the state Supreme Court if the appellate court upholds the decision again.

Prosecutor Ronn Couillard, assistant district attorney for Tulare County, disagreed with Simonian. He said the decision to introduce the Bibbee case was proper, and he said he doesn't understand why Bibbee's murder has gone uncharged for so long.

"I feel that it was a just verdict," Couillard said. "Now, I wish Fresno would file its case."

Visalia Times-Delta, December 17, 1985.

Letters

Mad at Stone verdict

Editor, Times-Delta:

The D.A. is so anxious to further his political career to a judgeship that he is compromising the integrity of the justice system in our country.

Ronn Couillard told the jury to disregard the sworn testimony of three of his own witnesses who have cleared David Stone of the charges brought against him if the truth were used.

1. Couillard advised the jury to discount the sworn testimony of Dr. Morrison, the pathologist who established the time of death for the homocide as 10 p.m., Saturday, Oct. 6, 1979. David and his wife were in Las Vegas at that time with proof of this before the court.

2. Couillard advised the jury to discount the sworn testimony of Lonnie Powers, who identified a specific person as "the man from Fresno" (NOT David Stone) who bought the Krugerrands and was coming back on Saturday to buy thousands of dollars more from Mr. Moyer, the deceased. David Stone was accused by the D.A. of being "the man from Fresno" who bought the Krugerrands and with no proof of such evidence.

3. Couillard told the jury to discount the sworn testimony of Joe Diaz, the postman who delivered mail to Mr. Moyer's shop at 10:45 a.m., Saturday morning, Oct. 6, 1979 and no mail was found on the floor Sunday morning by the police department here. Diaz said he dropped the mail through the slot in the shop's door. David and his wife were in Fresno with proof at 10:58 a.m. that day. Who picked up the mail on Saturday? Couillard theorized Mr. Moyer was killed at 10 a.m. Saturday.

Judge Ballantyne and the D.A., Ronn Couillard acted in concert to influence the jury to convict David Stone. As Judge Hansen of the 5th District Appeal Court said of the first trial in her opinion, that "the strained logic and questionable inferences in this case are obvious." David Stone was convicted with no proof. Only strained logic and questionable inferences, and a clever way of influencing the jury to substantiate the theory of what happened as so determined by the judge and the D.A. This method of conducting a trial is a disgrace to our judicial system. Subverting the truth of sworn witnesses' testimony to accomplish one's own "theory" (Couillard's) should not be permitted.

This, at the sentencing by Judge Ballantyne for David E. Stone, 27 years to life.

Eston E. Stone, Jr.
Visalia

Letters

Disagrees with Stone

Editor:

This is a response to Eston E. Stone Jr.'s letter in the Jan. 25 issue of the Times-Delta.

Your letter accuses District Attorney Ronn Couillard of compromising our justice system. You base your accusation on the fact that the DA, during his closing argument, instructed the jury to disregard the testimony of three witnesses. Your accusation is ludicrous.

Mr. Stone, closing arguments are NOT evidence. Judge Ballantyne admonished the jury of this fact. Closing arguments are an opportunity for each attorney to tell the jury what they believe the correct interpretation of the evidence should be. During this stage, favorable evidence is highlighted while damaging evidence is either explained, downplayed, or ignored. The jury has the power to accept or reject any contention made by the attorney during the closing argument. A verdict is based on evidence presented at trial, not closing arguments.

The DA acted well within his power when he requested the jury to downplay certain testimony.

Furthermore, he did not ask the jury to disregard any testimony. He simply asked the jury to give the testimony the weight that it deserved in light of other evidence that was presented during the trial. It was the jury who weighed the evidence, not Mr. Couillard. It was the jury who found David Stone guilty of first-degree murder, not Mr. Couillard.

Mr. Stone, do you believe that it was proper for your son's first defense attorney to use his closing argument to accuse an innocent third party of murder, after he failed during the trial to bring forth one shred of evidence to support that accusation? Speaking of injustice!

While speaking of injustices, there is something inherently wrong when a convicted murderer is given a new trial based on new evidence and not one piece of that new evidence justified a new trial. If it did, then why wasn't it used?

You next contend that your son was convicted with no proof, "only strained logic and questionable inferences."

Yet, there have been two trials, two different defense attorneys, two different juries, and two unanimous guilty verdicts. No proof?

Accusing the DA and the judge of acting in concert to influence the jury to convict your son is a gross misstatement of the truth. Only truth and the hard work and competence of DA Ronn Couillard served to keep a dangerous killer from being set free.

David A. Dye
Visalia

Left: Eston Stone letter to the editor. *From the* Visalia Times-Delta.

Right: Letter to the editor in response to Eston Stone's letter. *From the* Visalia Times-Delta.

make the defense's position looked contrived at best. It was after this decision that David took the witness stand and told his story. This was not a good day for the defense.

We concluded closing arguments on Friday, December 14, and the jury retired to deliberate late that afternoon. The members were released by Judge Ballantyne at 5:00 p.m. and asked to return Monday to continue their deliberations. Shortly after noon that Monday, they returned with a verdict of guilty of murder in the first degree. Upon the verdict being read by the court clerk, Betsy Stone began sobbing loudly. David, who appeared noticeably annoyed at the verdict, turned around and told her, "I expected it."

On January 13, 1986, David Stone was once again sentenced to state prison for the murder of Frank Alexander Moyer Jr.

David Stone's appeal of the second trial was denied, the conviction was affirmed and David set his sights on different and more ingenious methods of overturning his conviction. According to a front-page article in the *Daily Journal*, a legal newspaper for the state of California, David's appellate attorney, "while reviewing the file [Stone's inmate file at Soledad Prison] for information that might be useful in securing a new trial," supposedly discovered a memorandum purportedly signed by the director of the Department of Corrections and addressed to the warden at the Soledad Prison facility. The memorandum, written on official State Corrections Department letterhead, was dated December 4, 1989, and stamped received on January 23, 1990, by the warden's office.

The content of the memorandum was most interesting, especially to me. In the body of the memorandum appeared the following: "The District Attorney who was in charge of the prosecution of this individual, is now of the opinion that Stone was not responsible for the commitment offense for which he is now incarcerated. However, due to other considerations, his office is not willing at this time to pursue the matter further." The director stated that neither he nor his secretary wrote the memo, and he said the signature that purported to be his was a forgery. No prison official claimed prior knowledge of the memo, nor could they state how it got into Stone's prison file.

When contacted by the newspaper, I emphatically stated that I had no doubt about David's guilt of the Moyer murder (the commitment offense), had never communicated otherwise and added that I was convinced he also

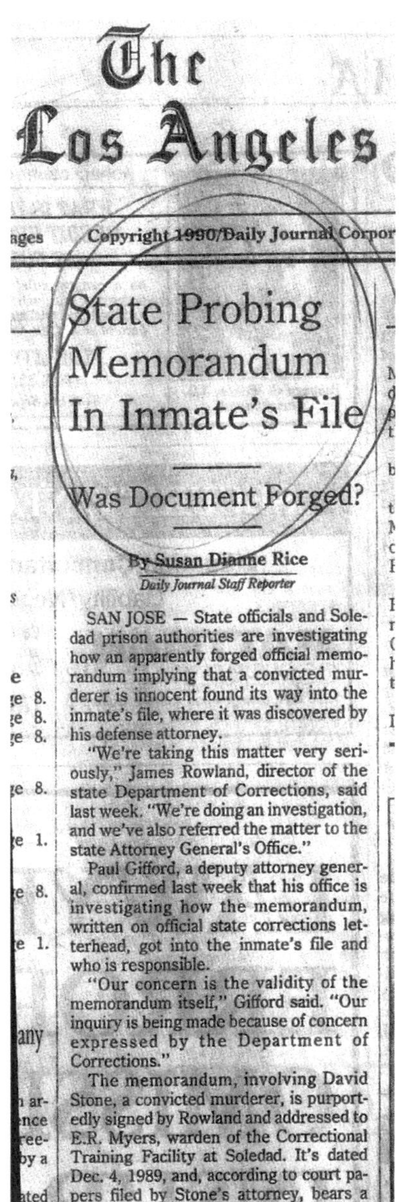

The Los Angeles

Copyright 1990/Daily Journal Corpor

State Probing Memorandum In Inmate's File

Was Document Forged?

By Susan Dianne Rice
Daily Journal Staff Reporter

SAN JOSE — State officials and Soledad prison authorities are investigating how an apparently forged official memorandum implying that a convicted murderer is innocent found its way into the inmate's file, where it was discovered by his defense attorney.

"We're taking this matter very seriously," James Rowland, director of the state Department of Corrections, said last week. "We're doing an investigation, and we've also referred the matter to the state Attorney General's Office."

Paul Gifford, a deputy attorney general, confirmed last week that his office is investigating how the memorandum, written on official state corrections letterhead, got into the inmate's file and who is responsible.

"Our concern is the validity of the memorandum itself," Gifford said. "Our inquiry is being made because of concern expressed by the Department of Corrections."

The memorandum, involving David Stone, a convicted murderer, is purportedly signed by Rowland and addressed to E.R. Myers, warden of the Correctional Training Facility at Soledad. It's dated Dec. 4, 1989, and, according to court papers filed by Stone's attorney, bears a

Forged document found in David Stone's prison file. *From the* Los Angeles Daily Journal.

murdered a coin dealer in Fresno a few months earlier (the Bibee murder) for which he had not yet been prosecuted. Just as importantly, I informed them that I was the only one within the Tulare County District Attorney's office who handled the Moyer case and thus no other attorney would have cause to make such comments.

This somewhat amateurish ploy by David Stone, along with whomever he had employed to "spring" him from prison, failed. However, a more brazen attempt was made some years later. There surfaced, again through Stone's appellate attorney, a one-page police report dated late 1980 in which Bill McGowen had purportedly interviewed one of Alex Moyer's customers named George Greer. In the interview, Mr. Greer supposedly made statements about some concerns Moyer had of being robbed by a certain customer of his—not David Stone. In the report, there was a statement that the prosecutor (allegedly me) had told McGowen to keep this report confidential and not reveal the information to the defense.

Obviously, this was not true. McGowen had interviewed a George Greer, but Mr. Greer could give no meaningful information about either the murder or any suspicious persons. Further, I had never told any police investigator to keep any reports, contents of interviews or any other information confidential. Investigation of this bogus document revealed that it

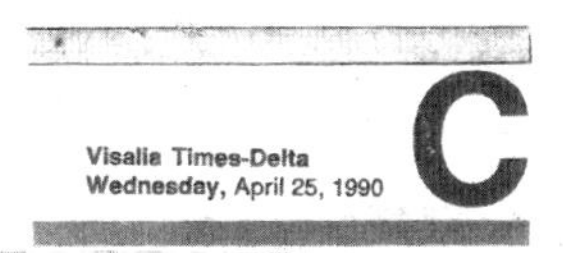

Visalia Times-Delta
Wednesday, April 25, 1990

C

Visalia judge denies murder verdict doubts

Prisons chief says document was forged

Associated Press

SALINAS — A Tulare County Municipal Court judge has denied a report that he believed a man he helped convict in a Visalia murder was innocent. The state prisons chief says the document is a forgery.

Judge Ronn Couillard, who was the prosecutor in the case that sent David Stone to prison for 27 years to life, said, "In no way have I ever had any doubts about his [Stone's] guilt." He said he was the only one in the Tulare County District Attorney's office who handled the case.

Stone was sentenced in the 1979 murder of a Visalia coin dealer.

Stone's lawyer has asked the Monterey County Superior Court to order release of the document for Stone's bid for a new trial.

According to papers filed with the court by attorney Cliff Gardner, the document, on state Department of Corrections letterhead, reads in part:

"The district attorney who was in charge of the prosecution of this individual is now of the opinion that Stone was not responsible for the commitment offense for which he is now incarcerated. However, due to other considerations, his office is not willing at this time to pursue the matter further."

The document says it was

See Guilt/2C

DAY

Guilt

Continued from page 1C

written Dec. 4 by state Corrections Director James Rowland to E.R. Myers, warden of the state prison at Soledad, where Stone is now held.

But the San Francisco Banner Daily Journal on Monday quoted both Rowland and Couillard as denying the contents of the document.

"That memo was not written by me or by my secretary," Rowland said. "It was on department letterhead, but it was not my signature. I have no idea how it got into [Stone's] file."

He said his department and the state attorney general's office were investigating the matter.

Stone has insisted all along that he was innocent of the murder. His first conviction in 1982 was overturned because of newly discovered evidence, but he was convicted again in a second trial, and the conviction was upheld on appeal.

Gardner said he found the memo in the non-confidential portion of Stone's prison file April 5, although it was marked for the confidential file. He said he wrote down the contents after prison officials refused to give him a copy.

Reporting forged document found in David Stone's prison file. *From the* Visalia Times-Delta.

was the last page of a multi-page report on which there were only a few words and that it had been turned over to the defense along with all other reports as part of the discovery process. Upon closer examination and comparison to the original report, it became clear that some white-outs had occurred, and some new information was inserted. The page had been altered to look like the report contained statements by Mr. Greer naming a potential suspect. It was obviously a phony. The matter was submitted to the California Attorney General's Office for further investigation. Whether an investigation was ever conducted or not, I have no knowledge.

Just as with the phony prison document, this report was a forgery and a futile attempt by the David Stone camp to overturn his second murder conviction. I have no knowledge if the California State Bar ever looked into these matters with respect to the appellate attorney. However, one could logically conclude that he could well have had some complicity in these efforts since he caused them to surface, and it was obvious that David Stone would need some assistance in putting forth these false documents.

Meanwhile, David Stone, the convicted killer of Alex Moyer and the suspected yet unprosecuted killer of James Bibee, awaits eligibility for parole.

POSTSCRIPT

Bill Wittman and I became friends during the years of prosecuting David Stone and remained friends after the Stone case was concluded. We both had changes in our respective careers.

I was appointed as a judge in Tulare County in June 1987. I retired in July 2007 but served on assignment on a part-time basis until September 2016. In 1995, Wittman was elected sheriff of Tulare County and stepped down as sheriff in 2013 due to health reasons.

In early December 2010, I received a telephone call from Sheriff Wittman during which he gave me the most startling news. He said he had just been contacted by Betsy Stone, and she told him she wanted to meet with the both of us. This was like a "bolt out of the blue," as neither of us had any contact with her since the last trial exactly twenty-five years earlier. I had never spoken to her, as she made it a point to avoid me, I'm sure under the direction of David's parents. Although Bill had questioned her on a few occasions, she had been very guarded and uncooperative. This request had both of us curious, although she did tell Wittman in her telephone call that she was concerned because David was due for a parole hearing.

A meeting was scheduled in Wittman's office for early January. She arrived accompanied by her brother. The Betsy Stone we met with looked like the Betsy Stone I remembered from twenty-five years before. She, of course, had aged somewhat, but her hair was the same brownish-blond, with just a few touches of gray. Her face was much as I remembered it, with one exception: she smiled a lot. I remember her in the past as always looking sullen and almost frightened and being noticeably nervous. The Betsy Stone we encountered that day in January 2011 was smiling and readily engaged in conversation.

She divorced David shortly after his last commitment to prison and had remarried. The purpose of her requesting the meeting was an upcoming parole hearing for David. That hearing was scheduled for the following February, some thirteen months away. She flat out told us that she was "scared for her life if David were released." She went on to explain that he had threatened her when the divorce was taking place and further threatened her should she ever remarry.

She also said that both the children, the young daughter whose birthday was being celebrated at the time of the Bibee murder and a boy with whom she was pregnant at the Moyer trial, had been in contact with their father. To her understanding, they were going to ask for his being released on parole. I got the impression, listening to her, that there was some tension between her and the children regarding their contact with their father. As she related to us, "They only know what he has told them," and of course, he had them convinced he was not guilty of either murder. In her opinion, they were only believing what they wanted to believe.

She then asked us about parole hearing proceedings and who could have input. We informed her that any interested party could appear and/or have written input. We assured her that we would both write letters opposing any release and that the Tulare County District Attorney's Office always sends an attorney to what are referred to as "lifer hearings." I also informed her that it is extremely rare for anyone convicted of murder to be released on parole. Further, to even be considered for such release, the inmate must genuinely confess to responsibility for the murder, something that we all agreed David Stone would never do.

After we discussed the parole situation, I asked Betsy if she would discuss the events involving the Bibee and Moyer murders. She agreed and, in fact, indicated that she had wanted to in the past but was too frightened to do so. She also told us that David's parents, who were basically supporting her at the time, prevented her from doing so. She said that they never verbally threatened her but nonetheless never let her out of their sight and scrutinized every move she made. What she told us was what Wittman and I had suspected all the time.

On Thursday, August 2, 1979, she had, in fact, driven to Le Grand with her young daughter to visit her parents. She and David had only one car at the time, the one owned by Eston Stone, and she drove it that day. She left at about midday and did not return until sometime after dark, which in August would be around 9:00 p.m. When she returned home, she drove the car into the garage and sensed that something wrong immediately upon getting out of the car. As she told us, "I could sense something, I could actually smell something was wrong." Curiously, she used the word *smell* although, as she explained, it wasn't truly a smell but such a strong feeling that "I thought I smelled something was wrong, if that makes any sense."

The garage was attached to the house, and upon entering the door to the house, she told us that this "smell" or feeling became even stronger. She knew something had happened and asked David about it. He indicated that there was nothing wrong. However, she said her concerns were strengthened when the police started calling the next day. She stated that David told her about Mr. Bibee's disappearance and that he was the last one to see Bibee that evening. That was when he induced her to say she was at the house while he and Mr. Bibee traded coins and that Bibee left sometime around six o'clock.

She said that she was scared and confused and allowed herself to be intimidated by David. Because of this, she had knowingly lied to the police by following her husband's instructions. Betsy then stated that the reason she failed to appear in the first trial to testify to this story is that she knew she would be under oath and was afraid to testify falsely. She then told us that if the Bibee murder were to be prosecuted, she would testify to the events of that day because, as she said, "In my heart I know he killed Mr. Bibee."

That day I saw a much different Betsy Stone from who I remembered. Rather than appearing nervous and intimidated, she was relaxed, confident and self-assured. She could not, or would not, give much information about the morning of the Moyer murder. She said that it was David's idea to stay at a motel in town the night before, and when she awoke that morning, he was gone. When he returned, he said he had taken the car to get gas and to "be checked over" before their journey to Las Vegas. Then they checked out and started their trip.

We concluded our discussions and agreed to meet again before the date of the parole hearing. As it turned out, another meeting was not necessary. David Stone died of natural causes about four months later. So ended the story of the coin dealer murders.

TIMELINE

1978

December 28—Jewelry store armed robbery in Fresno.

1979

August 2—Fresno coin dealer James Bibee disappears.

August 7—James Bibee's body is found in the trunk of his car parked in front of the Clovis Police Department.

October 6—Visalia coin dealer Alex Moyer is murdered in his Visalia coin shop.

October 7—Alex Moyer's body is discovered by neighbors.

1980

April 1—David Stone is arrested for the Fresno jewelry store robbery.

April 2—David Stone posts bail and is released from custody.

April 29—Handwritten price tag is found under David Stone's house in Fresno.

May 27—Preliminary hearing is held on the Fresno robbery charge; David Stone is ordered to stand trial.

October 16—David Stone is arrested for Alex Moyer murder.

October 20—David Stone is released, with no charges filed.

1981

January 12—David Stone's Fresno jewelry robbery trial starts.

January 14—David Stone absconds from trial at noon break.

January 14—Alex Moyer murder charges are filed against David Stone in Visalia.

January 15—David Stone returns to court and is remanded; parties waive jury, and court finds him guilty of armed robbery.

February 13—David Stone is sentenced to five years in state prison.

February 17—David Stone is arrested for the murder of Alex Moyer.

August—Preliminary hearing is held on the Alex Moyer murder charge; David Stone is ordered to stand trial.

1982

March 22—David Stone's murder trial begins.

April 2—Final arguments begin in murder trial.

April 8—David Stone is found guilty of the murder of Alex Moyer.

May 6—David Stone is sentenced to twenty-seven years to life in state prison.

1984

February 22—Appellate Court overturns conviction for murder of Alex Moyer and grants new trial.

1985

December 3—Second David Stone murder trial begins.

December 17—David Stone is found guilty for the murder of Alex Moyer.

1986

January 13—David Stone is sentenced to twenty-seven years to life in state prison.

INDEX

V

W

Z

ABOUT THE AUTHOR

Ronn Couillard has worked in the criminal justice system in California since 1968, when he began as a deputy district attorney for Los Angeles County. In June 1980, he moved to Visalia and served as a deputy district attorney for Tulare County. He was appointed to the Tulare County Superior Court in July 1987. After retiring in 2007, he continued as an assigned judge until September 2016. In the past forty-eight years, he has both prosecuted and presided over all types of felony matters, including numerous murder cases. He and his wife, Charlotte, reside in Visalia, California. They have four grown children and seven grandchildren.

Visit us at
www.historypress.net

This title is also available as an e-book